JOSHUA TREE NATIONAL PARK

THE INSIDER'S GUIDE

ROBERT MIRAMONTES

Joshua Tree National Park: The Insider's Guide

Author: Robert Miramontes.

Maps: Robert Miramontes.

Photographs: Miramontes Photography, unless otherwise credited.

Published and distributed by Wolverine Publishing, LLC.

Cover photo: Lost Horse Road area. Inset: Thunderstorm in the Park. Miramontes Photography.

Opening page photo:

Dwarf juniper at Jumbo Rocks Campground. Miramontes Photography.

International Standard Book Number:

ISBN: 978-1-938393-23-5

Library of Congress Catalog in Publication data:

Library of Congress Catalog Control Number: 9781938393235

Wolverine Publishing is continually expanding its range of guidebooks. If you have a manuscript or idea for a book, or would like to find out more about our company and publications, contact:

Wolverine Publishing

PO Box 195

New Castle, CO 81652

970-876-0269

www.wolverinepublishing.com

Printed in Korea

Preface

This book was created with the vision of introducing the casual visitor to the subtle yet profound beauty of Joshua Tree National Park, and to inspire you with beautiful images. The vastness of the Park can be overwhelming, and the details easy to overlook; we hope to help you see them. Within these pages you will discover major points of interest, hidden attractions, numerous hikes of all lengths and difficulties, and a variety of other activities to do while visiting the area. We hope that the imagery will stir your imagination and spark a child-like desire to get out of the car and explore the infinite nooks and crannies in Joshua Tree National Park.

WARNING

DO NOT USE THIS GUIDEBOOK UNLESS YOU READ AND AGREE TO THE FOLLOWING:

Hiking and scrambling can be dangerous and can result in death or serious injury.

Some of the hikes and scrambles described in this book traverse potentially hazardous terrain. Even marked trails may have dangerous drops, and off-trail routes may require difficult scrambling where a fall could result in injury or death. This book relies upon information gathered by the author about terrain that is not only potentially hazardous, but also subject to change. Trails or cross-country routes may deteriorate, boulders may shift, and wet or icy conditions may exist that render the routes highly dangerous. Furthermore, errors may be made during the editing, designing, proofing, and printing of this book. Thus, the information in this book is unverified, and the authors and publisher cannot guarantee its accuracy. Numerous hazards exist that are not described in this book. Traveling on any terrain described in this book, regardless of its description or rating, may result in injury.

Do not use this book unless you understand and accepts the risks. If you choose to use any information in this book to attempt a particular route, you do so at your own risk. Please take all precautions and use your own ability, evaluation, and judgment to assess the risks of your chosen route, rather than solely relying on the information in this book.

Milky Way rising over an eerie landscape of Joshua trees.

TABLE OF CONTENTS

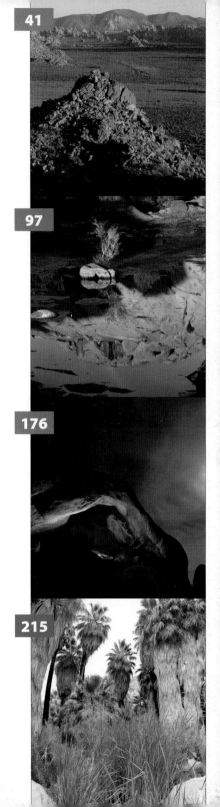

41

97

176

215

A late-summer thunderstorm in Lost Horse Valley.

INTRODUCTION

Joshua Tree National Park — A quixotic landscape of rock and shadow, of Dr. Seuss, Beetlejuice, Freud, and Poe. A strange world filled with subtle beauty, stark adversity, and grand complexity. At a glance, the small rock formations and sprawls of open desert may make Joshua Tree seem dull compared to other national parks such as Yosemite or Zion with their soaring cliffs and spectacular waterfalls. Joshua Tree requires that one slow down a bit, step out of the car, and walk away from the pavement—maybe scramble around on the plethora of rocks, or just sit quietly under a piñon pine and listen.

Whether you're looking for a rugged wilderness adventure or just a Sunday drive, Joshua Tree has something for you. The most casual visitor can drive to overlooks with grand vistas, or take a short nature walk on a manicured trail. For those looking to get away from the car, there are more lengthy hikes on well-marked trails. For the most adventurous, there are cross-country hikes and even steep scrambles to the summits of rocky formations, as well as challenging desert peaks to climb.

Mining and history enthusiasts will be treated to some of the finest turn-of-the-century mining equipment and structures to be found within the entire national park system. Many of these sites are integrated into beautiful landscapes, largely reclaimed by nature. Others appear as if their occupants left just yesterday. Some sites are completely off the tourist radar, accessible only to the savvy hiker who knows where to go.

For bird and animal watchers, there's an abundance of wildlife: 250 species of birds are found in the Park, as well as 52 species of mammals and over 40 species of reptiles. Several species are considered threatened or endangered, including the Desert Tortoise and the Desert Bighorn Sheep.

And finally, the night sky! It's not uncommon for stargazers to flock to Joshua Tree National Park during seasonal meteor showers or to view the Milky Way at its peak. Astronomy clubs will occasionally set up telescopes in Park parking lots, encouraging visitors to come have a peek.

LOCATION

Joshua Tree National Park sits just outside the town of Joshua Tree in the high desert of Southern California, roughly 100 miles east of Los Angeles and about 40 miles north of Palm Springs. Interstate 10 is the closest major freeway. See map on page 32.

West Entrance: This is the best option if coming from the LA area, San Diego area, or from the vicinity of Palm Springs. From Interstate 10, take HWY 62 north for 27 miles to Park Boulevard. Turn right (S) onto Park Boulevard. The West Entrance Visitors Center is about 300 yards ahead, on the right. Continue 5.2 miles to reach the West Entrance. There is a fee station at the entrance, where limited information can be obtained. Restrooms and running water can also be found here. See map on page 32.

North Entrance: The best entrance if traveling from the 29 Palms Marine Base, Las Vegas, or from the Colorado River area. Travel HWY 62 to the town of 29 Palms. Continue to the east side of town, turning south onto Utah Trail (or National Park Drive, which ends at Utah Trail). The North Entrance Visitors Center is located at the corner of Utah Trail and National Park Drive. Continue south on Utah Trail for 3.5 miles to the North Entrance. There is a fee station at the entrance, where limited information can be obtained. Restrooms can also be found here. See map on page 32.

South Entrance: This is a good option if coming from the Indio/Coachella Valley area or from Arizona on Interstate 10. From Interstate 10 (24.2 miles east of Indio, approximately 75 miles west of the Arizona border), turn north on Cottonwood Spring Road. The Park boundary is just over a mile away, but there is no entrance station here. The nearest facility is Cottonwood Visitors Center, another 6 miles along the road. At the center, visitors can pay the entrance fee, obtain free information on the Park, and also purchase Joshua Tree related items from the bookstore. Restrooms and picnic tables can also be found here. See map on page 32.

MAP
OF
CALIFORNIA

N

San Francisco

Bishop

395

Joshua Tree National Park

Los Angeles

Palm Springs

62

San Diego

The popular West Entrance on a busy morning.

ENTERING
JOSHUA TREE
NATIONAL PARK
UNITED STATES DEPARTMENT OF THE INTERIOR
NATIONAL PARK SERVICE

Indian Cove: This secluded cove lies on the northern border of Joshua Tree National Park, cut off from the rest of the Park by the Queen Mountain Range and the massive Wonderland of Rocks. Indian Cove is located off of HWY 62, between the town of Joshua Tree (9.2 miles) and 29 Palms (5.7 miles). Turn south onto Indian Cove Road and drive 1 mile to the entrance station. Restrooms and information can be found here. See map on page 32.

Black Rock Campground: Found just south of the town of Yucca Valley, at the western-most tip of Joshua Tree National Park. Take HWY 62 to the middle of town. Turn south onto Joshua Lane and drive 4.8 miles to the campground entrance. The visitors center is found in the middle of the campground. See map on page 32.

PARK ENTRY FEES

Prices are subject to change, and do so often!
- $30 - per vehicle (7-day pass)
- $25 - per motorcycle (7-day)
- $15 - bicycle or walk-in (7-day)
- $55 - Joshua Tree annual pass
- $80 - National Park annual pass
- $20 - Senior Citizen annual National Park pass
- Free - Disabled or blind

EMERGENCY

Cell service is very limited in the Park. There is an emergency phone located at Intersection Rock parking lot, at the restroom. Otherwise, the next closest contact is at one of the entrance stations. Call 911 or the Park Dispatcher at (909) 383-5651.

AMENITIES

Three towns lie in close proximity to Joshua Tree National Park along HWY 62, north of the Park. They are Twenty-Nine Palms, Joshua Tree, and Yucca Valley. See map on page 32.

Twenty-Nine Palms

This growing town is located approximately 5 miles north of the North Entrance, and reasonably close to the Park. You'll find all the standard accommodations, including several gas

ONLY HAVE A FEW HOURS?

If you're visiting the Park but only have a couple of hours, here are some options to maximize your time. Depending on which direction you are coming from, try these quick excursions:

West Entrance: Probably the best way to see the Park is to drive from the West Entrance to the North Entrance (or vice versa), making a return loop on HWY 62. This can be done in 2 hours or less. Many convenient parking lots, restrooms, and turnouts can be accessed on the drive. If in the vicinity of Yucca Valley, consider checking out the High View Trail at Black Rock Campground: it's only a 10-minute drive from the center of town, and the trail can be walked in 1 hour.

North Entrance: Visitors coming from the vicinity of 29 Palms may want to check out the 49 Palms Oasis parking lot. The drive in passes through some beautiful scenery, and the parking lot itself has excellent vistas of 29 Palms and the desert beyond. It's also possible to walk just the first third of the 49 Palms Oasis trail (a casual 1-hour round trip), which winds through rock piles, ascending briskly to a mountain ridge with beautiful vistas and occasional peeks of the oasis in the distance. Another option from the North Entrance is to drive 0.5 miles and park at a turnout with an information board, then walk the trail leaving from the board, heading to nearby rock piles a short distance away.

South Entrance: If you're traveling along the Interstate 10, it is possible to stop in and take a quick hike or just sightsee. The short Bajada Trail is only 1.5 miles from the freeway, and has a restroom. You could be back on the freeway in 40 minutes. If you have 2 hours to explore, then continue on to Cottonwood Springs. Check out the Visitors Center and ejnoy a short nature trail, or head to Cottonwood Spring and take the short paved trail among the shimmering cottonwood trees and fan palms.

stations, hotels from small and inexpensive to large and pricey, a supermarket, small markets, restaurants, and fast food.

Hotel 29 Palms
71809 29 Palms Hwy
(760) 361-4009; nathsons.com

Fairfield Inn and Suites
6333 Encilia Ave
(760) 361-5000; marriot.com

Twenty-Nine Palms Inn
73950 Inn Ave
(760) 367-3505; 29palmsinn.com

Best Western Inn and Suites
71487 29 Palms Hwy
(760) 367-9141; bestwesterncalifornia.com

Edchadas Mexican Restaurant
7305 29 Palms Hwy
(760) 367-2131

Bistro Twenty Nine
73527 29 Palms Hwy
(760) 361-2229; bistrotwentynine.com

Joshua Tree

This small town is approximately 5 miles north of the West Entrance. The junction with Highway 62 and Park Boulevard is more or less the center of town. Many small, interesting stores can be found in this little area, from hiking supply to old bookstores, from arts and crafts to hippy outposts. There is also a gas station, several small cafes, and a couple of bars.

Nomad Ventures (hiking gear)
61795 29 Palms Hwy
(760) 366-4684

Coyote Corner (hiking gear)
6535 Park Blvd
(760) 366-9683

Crossroads Cafe and Tavern
61715 29 Palms Hwy
(760) 366-5414; crossroadscafeandtavern.com

High Desert Motel
61310 29 Palms Hwy
(760) 366-1978; magnusonhotels.com

Joshua Tree Inn
61259 29 Palms Hwy
(760) 366-1188; joshuatreeinn.com

Safari Motor Inn
61959 29 Palms Hwy
(760) 366-1113;
joshuatreemotel.com

Yucca Valley

The largest of the three towns near the Park, Yucca Valley is located about 8 miles west of the town of Joshua Tree on Highway 62. Yucca Valley has all the standard accommodations including gas stations, hotels, supermarkets, restaurants, fast food, and even department stores.

Winter in the Park.

Maelstrom: Star tails over Covington Flats with passing thunderstorms in the distance.

WEATHER

The primary seasons to visit Joshua Tree are fall, winter, and spring. After the heat of summer, the Park starts to get "good" around mid-September, although there may be many hot days through the end of October. After that, it's usually nice until about mid-April, when uncomfortably hot days start to creep back in. The Park may then see some cool days until June, after which the norm is around 100° F. The lower elevation areas—Pinto Basin, Pleasant Valley, and Indian Cove—all tend to be warmer. Upper Covington Flats and Black Rock Canyon are the coolest areas in the Park.

Fall: Average highs 60° to 85°. Occasional thunderstorms.

Winter: Average daytime highs 50° to 75°. Perfect weather is the norm, but high winds can make even sunny days very cold. Nighttime temps can plummet to below zero! Occasional snowstorms can shut the whole place down—towns and all. Snow usually only lasts on the ground for a few days.

Spring: Average daytime temps hover around 60° to 80°. Mostly perfect weather all season. Beautiful wildflower displays! You may still get occasional "freak" snowstorms.

Summer: Average temps around 90° to 105°. Cumulus build-ups and occasional thunderstorms are common. Typically, it's too hot to be out and about in the Park during midday hours, though it's possible to have occasional nice days. Mornings and late afternoons can sometimes be pleasant. Even the nights can be unpleasantly hot in summer, with temps often lingering in the low 90s.

Joshua Tree Regulations

Litter: Obviously, littering is illegal! This includes cigarette butts, orange peels, banana peels, eggshells, and toilet paper. Please be responsible and pack out everything you bring. Trashcans can be found at most parking lots.

Dogs: All pets must be leashed at all times in the Park. No exceptions! Pets are prohibited on trails and may NEVER be taken more than 50 feet from a road, picnic area, or campground. Pets cannot be left unattended—not even in a car. See below for more information on dogs.

Wildlife: Feeding wild animals (including coyotes, squirrels, and birds) is illegal. All wildlife in Joshua Tree National Park is protected by law.

Souvenirs: Removing anything from the park is illegal. This includes rocks, cactus, wood, old tin cans, lizards, etc.

DOGS

Surprisingly, bringing a dog to Joshua Tree National Park is not the best idea. Impact laws restrict domestic pets to within 50 feet of designated roads. Dogs are not allowed on any trails. Dogs are not allowed in the open desert. Dogs must be leashed at all times. Furthermore, dogs are not allowed to be locked in the car and left alone, not even in the middle of winter! All this means that if you bring your dog, you too are restricted to roads and parking lots.

There are options. Many less-traveled dirt roads can found throughout the Park, any of which could make for an excellent outing. If in central Joshua Tree, consider parking at Barker Dam and walking the dirt road that branches off just before the parking lot (this is the dirt portion of Bighorn Pass Road). It's also possible to drive this road a bit and park at one of several turnouts, walking from there. This road travels for miles through a pass and across the open desert, even splitting into two roads for more options. Visitors coming in from the North Entrance may want to visit the Live Oak Picnic Area; dogs allowed.

Driving: Speed limits are enforced here. Also, driving off established roads is prohibited.

Off-Roading: Driving off-road is not permitted in the park. ATVs and other non-street legal motorized vehicles are not permitted. All vehicle travel is restricted to established roads that are open to public access. See the Off-Roading section on page 22.

Bicycling: Biking is restricted to roads that are open to public access. Riding on trails, in washes, on open country, or anywhere "off road" is strictly prohibited. See biking section on page 20.

Campfires: Fires are permitted in campgrounds and picnic areas only, and only in the provided grated-pits and barbeques. Fires must be completely extinguished after use. Campfires are not allowed in the backcountry. Collecting wood or other vegetation, whether living or dead, is prohibited.

Food Storage: Food must be stored either in hard-sided plastic containers or in a vehicle to avoid attracting wild animals.

Overnight Parking: After-hours parking is allowed only in designated campsite lots, and at Backcountry Boards. Vehicles found unattended after 10 PM anywhere else will be ticketed.

Firearms: Firearms may be possessed in accordance with California state and federal laws; however they may not be used in the Park. BB guns, paintball guns, slingshots, bows, fireworks, and animal traps are prohibited.

Commercial Filming: A permit is required for filming or photography that involves advertising, the use of models, props, large equipment, etc.

Day-Use Areas

These pristine wilderness areas in Joshua Tree, officially known as Designated Wilderness Areas, have been set aside as wildlife refuge. Special restrictions must be observed when in these areas. The goal is to protect wildlife, including several endangered species, by reducing human disturbances in these select places. The areas typically involve prominent water sources, which the local wildlife depends on. As the name suggests, Day-Use Areas are only open during daylight hours. Visitors are expected to vacate the area by sunset. Camping or staying overnight within these boundaries is not permitted. Noise restrictions also apply in these areas. Violating Wilderness Area restrictions is a serious matter and could result in prosecution!

HAZARDS

Joshua Tree has some special dangers of which visitors should be aware. Of primary concern in the hotter seasons is dehydration. Always travel with plenty of water! In winter, be aware that temperatures after dark can plummet, so come prepared. Just about everything in the desert has some sort of barb or needle on it, from the mildly annoying Beavertail Cactus to the Yucca — potentially life-threatening should you fall on its spears!

Bees: Aggressive bees are common in Joshua Tree, usually in the hotter months. They are attracted to moisture — a sweaty shirt, an open drink, spilled water — and once they latch onto you, they don't seem to go away! Resist the urge to swat a bee down. An injured or dead bee can release a pheromone that alerts other bees to home in and take the offensive. If you're stung, it may be best to return to the car and roll up the windows. It's unclear whether the Park has true Africanized "killer bees," but it is not far from areas known to have them, and there have been aggressive swarm attacks reported. On rare occasions, usually in the spring, one may encounter a traveling swarm of bees. Typically these swarms are harmless, as the bees are focused on following the queen to a new home. (I wouldn't want to drive through a swarm with the top down, though!)

Rattlesnakes: These elusive creatures have the potential to inflict a life-threatening wound, and care should be taken to avoid them. A rattler would never seek out and attack a person. In fact, they usually avoid a confrontation at all costs, either freezing still, pretending to be a rock, or quietly slithering into the brush. If you do spook one, it may let you know with a loud buzzing from its rattle. If you get bitten, remain calm, and avoid activities that increase heart rate and blood flow. Get to a hospital as soon as possible.

A speckled rattlesnake blends into the landscape, frozen still on a cold winter day in the Wonderland of Rocks.

"What goes up, must come down". This balloon was probably released from a nearby city before coming to rest on this dead cholla in Lost Horse Valley.

MINIMIZING IMPACT

The desert is a harsh and unforgiving land, where only the heartiest survives its adversities. Life here hangs by very fragile threads. Joshua Tree supports several distinct ecosystems, some of which are the fading remnants of a wetter past. Damage to these delicate systems may take decades or even centuries to heal. Some of the environments here are considered non-regenerative, which is to say that once damaged they may never rebound from human impact. Note the many mining roads in the Park that can still be plainly seen even though they have not been driven on in 100 years!

The dusty old trails etched in the sand also reveal a foundation of desert life; cryptobiotic soil, a complex community of microorganisms living in the topsoil. These organisms break down minerals and plant matter, creating nutrients essential to plants. Without this process, plant life could not survive in the nutrient-devoid soils of this desert. Without plant cover, erosion accelerates and removes even more of the precious topsoil. When hiking in Joshua Tree, preserving cryptobiotic soils should be a primary concern, best achieved by staying on the trails or by walking in washes or on rock surfaces.

Joshua Tree is also home to several endangered and/or protected animals, including the Desert Bighorn Sheep and Desert Tortoise. Disturbing these creatures should be avoided at all costs (and any person caught disturbing wildlife within the Park will be prosecuted). Please respect any posted closures and carefully read the rules and regulations regarding wildlife.

Trash is another problem that impacts the desert. It's illegal, it's unsightly, and it disrupts wildlife. Coyote, Desert Tortoises, and other critters have been known to ingest trash, sometimes with lethal results. Here are a few tips to help keep trash to a minimum:
• When picnicking, keep napkins and other light items contained. Sudden gusts of wind, squirrels, and coyotes have been known to sweep items off a table and carry them into the desert.
• Keep loose trash and wrappers inside of vehicles contained. A common scenario is to open the car

door and have a gust of wind pull trash out of the car, carrying it off into the desert faster than it can be retrieved.

• Fires are allowed in fire pits only, and collecting vegetation or wood is strictly prohibited.

• Please do not release helium balloons in the desert (or anywhere else, for that matter); they tend to fly off to remote areas of the wilderness and then land. Tortoises and other creatures can become entangled in the strings.

• Cigarette butts, egg shells, fruit peels, climbers tape, and used toilet paper should be disposed of in one of the many trashcans to be found in parking lots throughout the park.

CAMPING

Joshua Tree National Park boasts nine campgrounds, totaling nearly 500 sites. Unfortunately, this does not guarantee you'll find an empty site! The Park is a very popular camping destination, and most all of the sites are on a first-come, first-served basis, with the exception of Black Rock and Indian Cove. Reservations can be made for Black Rock and Indian Cove from October through May, up to six months in advance. Also note that in off-seasons, several of the campgrounds are closed.

There are several group campgrounds found in the Park, at Indian Cove, Cottonwood, and Sheep Pass. Group campsites require reservations, which can be made up to 12 months in advance. A minimum occupancy of 10 people (maximum of 60 people per site) is also required. Group sites currently cost $30 per night.

For reservations or more information, call: (877) 444-6777. Check the Joshua Tree National Park website for more details www.nps.gov/jotr

• A $10 per day fee is required for most sites (Indian Cove, Black Rock, and Cottonwood cost $15 per day).

• A 14-day camping limit is enforced most of the year, and sites are limited to six people, three tents, and two cars. Cars parked outside site parking after-hours will be ticketed!

• Fires are allowed in fire pits only, and collecting vegetation or wood is strictly prohibited.

• Noise restrictions are enforced between 10 PM and 6 AM. This includes RV generators!

In Joshua Tree, "sleeping out under the stars" is the real thing!

- The Park offers no showers, RV hookups, or running water (with the exception of pay spigots at Black Rock campground, the West Entrance, and Cottonwood Visitors Center).

Hidden Valley Campground

This campground lies at the heart of central Joshua Tree. Sites here are nestled in amongst boulders and below towering rock piles. Endless hiking and exploring can be done from this location. The campground offers 44 sites total, all of which are first-come, first-served. The west side of the grounds is enclosed by an alcove within several large rock formations, offering cozy sites in a beautiful setting. The east side of the grounds is situated on the outside of the rock formations. Sites here offer a bit more privacy, as well as the open desert beyond for that wide-open feel. No running water. The National Park Service has been known to offer free "Climbers Coffee" in the mornings on peak-season weekends on the west side of the campground. See page 72 for more info on this campground.

Ryan Campground

This quaint little campground encircles two lonely rock piles sitting in a quiet corner of Lost Horse Valley. It has 31 sites, including one horse camp; all are first-come, first-served. No group or RV sites, no running water. The old Ryan Ranch is just a hop, skip, and jump away. A nearby rock formation called Headstone offers a bit of entertainment with an endless procession of rock climbers ascending its prows. The campground is also a waypoint along the epic California Riding and Hiking Trail. The horse camp makes an excellent launching point for riding the trail on horseback. See page page 117 for more info on this campground.

Sheep Pass Group Campground

This campground consists of six group campsites, available by reservation only. There are no individual sites available here. The campground is located on the northern toe of Ryan Mountain, in the pass, offering excellent views of both Lost Horse Valley and Queen Valley. The excellent Ryan Mountain Summit Trail extends to the entrance of the campground. See page page 127 for more info on this campground.

Jumbo Rocks Campground

Jumbo Rocks is a beautiful campground located on the eastern edge of the Mojave. The exposed bedrock here is scoured bare and deeply grooved, creating a haven of small alcoves, troughs, and corridors. The whole campground weaves through these alcoves, giving many of the sites a secluded feel. Jumbo Rocks has 124 sites, making it the largest campground in the Park. All sites are first-come, first-served. No running water. See page page 173 for more info on this campground.

Belle Campground

This pleasant little campground has 18 sites surrounding a large granite dome. The wide-open valley to the north offers pretty night views of the city lights of 29 Palms and the 29 Palms Marine Base. Strange lights are often seen in the hills behind 29 Palms. No running water. See page page 178 for more info on this campground.

White Tank Campground

Another pleasant little campground with just 15 sites scattered among strangely shaped rock spires and boulders. The beautiful Arch Rock can be found behind the campground. No running water. See page page 179 for more info on this campground.

Cottonwood Campground

This is the only campground in the eastern side of the park. Cottonwood Campground is a fairly large complex, containing 62 sites, three group sites, an RV dump, and running water. The Cottonwood Visitors Center is also within walking distance. Several major hikes and sights can be accessed from the campground, including the Winona Mill, Cottonwood Spring, Mastodon Mine, and the Lost Palms Oasis. See page page 202 for more info on this campground.

Indian Cove

This outstanding campground sits in the secluded Indian Cove, a niche in the northern front of the massive Wonderland of Rocks granite batholith. The 101 campsites plus 13 group sites sit around the base of towering rock piles. Several excellent hikes can be found near the grounds, and the massive rock piles behind the campground offer endless exploration. If you're not into climbing rock piles, there are also deep canyons and wide-open desert to enjoy. See page page 226 for more info on this campground.

Black Rock Campground

This rather large campground is the western-most destination in the Park, located in the hills above the town of Yucca Valley. Forests of juniper and piñon pine enclose the campground. Many hikes can be found around this site, including the unofficial start of the California Riding and Hiking Trail. Black Rock campground has 100 sites, including a horse camp. There is also a visitors center located in the middle of the grounds. Running water can be found here, and also an RV dump. See page page 216 for more info on this campground.

Backcountry Camping

With the exception of Designated Wilderness Areas, camping is allowed in Joshua Tree's backcountry. Campers must register at a Backcountry Board (forms provided at the boards) and must also leave their cars here (cars found outside these areas will be ticketed). There are 13 Backcountry Boards located throughout the Park: Black Rock Campground, Upper Covington Flats, Indian Cove, Wonderland North parking lot, Juniper Flats, Desert Queen Mine parking lot, Geology Tour Road, Pleasant Valley, North Entrance, Twin Tanks, Turkey Flats, Porcupine Wash, and Cottonwood.
The following requirements apply:

• Users must completely fill out the form provided.

• Overnight parking allowed at boards only.

• Camping must be at least one mile from the board, one mile from any road, and 500 feet from any trail.

• Fires are not allowed anywhere outside a campground fire pit. That is: No fires in the backcountry!

• Camping is expressly forbidden in Designated Wilderness Areas; all Wilderness boundaries are clearly outlined at the Backcountry Boards.

A backcountry registration board. This one is located at Black Rock Campground.

Enjoying the sunset and view from Covington Crest.

HIKING

Joshua Tree National Park is a mecca for hiking. The Park offers over 100 hikes, with everything from short paved walks alongside the parking lot, to long day hikes, to the multi-day, 35-mile California Riding and Hiking Trail. This book details just under 50 hikes, mainly focusing on easy to moderate one-day outings.

The established trails covered in this book vary in their degree of development. Some of the official trails are paved walkways with signs and fences to keep meanderers on course. Others are well-worn with occasional signs. Unofficial trails are much less developed, sometimes following old mine roads, climber trails, or game trails, typically with no signage or indications of where to go or how to get back. Some hikes just "wing it" cross-country, through the open desert or up obscure canyons, following the contours of the land to reach the objective.

Hikers can expect a wide variety of terrain. Most trails typically cross the open desert at some point. With hard-packed dirt and few obstacles other than patches of brush and Joshua trees, the hiking can be easy in these areas. Washes are a bit more difficult, usually involving some calf-burning travel through thick sand. In the mountainous areas of Joshua Tree, trails can get very steep and rocky, often following 100-year-old mine roads that are terribly eroded. Canyon travel usually involves sections of deep sand, as well as some sort of constriction, be it piles of boulders, dense brush, or both. Ascending a rock pile requires a bit of route finding, plotting a course over or between big boulders. Descending a rock pile is often harder than climbing it.

Hikers should come well prepared! Bring plenty of water and make sure to stop and drink it enroute. Carry a compass, and note the direction of the parking area after you start on an adventure. Hikers may also want to carry a jacket, even if it is warm out. Hot days can suddenly become cold after the sun drops below the horizon.

The Wonderland of Rocks is a unique place, with unique challenges for hikers, that are worthy of mention. To put it bluntly, it's really easy to get lost here! The Wonderland is a sea of boulder-covered peaks and boulder-filled canyons. Trail landmarks are easily lost in the monotonous backdrop, so hikers should consider their return path at all times. Resist the urge to shortcut through side canyons, as they often veer off in unexpected directions. Getting off course can result in frustrating boulder hopping trying to get back to a main trail.

As mentioned, the focus of this book is easy to moderate hikes that can be done in one day. Each chapter starts with a general description for the location, followed by descriptions of the hikes, as well as other activities and sights.

TRAIL INFORMATION BOXES. Hike descriptions begin with an information box that summarizes the hike's basic characteristics. This "at a glance" information includes:

Distance: Given in miles. Typically, this will be for the complete hike, including the return trip, and in most cases, the distance cited will be specifically explained in the Distance entry, to eliminate any doubt (for example: round trip, loop, or one-way). All distances have been calculated from satellite imagery.

Physical difficulty: A 1-5 rating of the overall difficulty of a hike, considering the length of the hike, elevation gains and losses, and also the demands of the terrain. A half-mile hike on a flat trail might get a rating of 1. A hike rated 5 might be 10 miles or more, with 1000 feet or more of elevation gain, and/or difficult terrain.

VISITING WITH CHILDREN?

This author recalls visiting Joshua Tree National Park as a young teen and being mesmerized by the endless rock piles to scramble on and explore. Now, as a parent, I see that same look in my three year-old daughter's eyes. The Park offers much to young explorers of all ages.

Visiting the Park with children is about as challenging as going just about anywhere with children. There are, however, a few challenges that are unique to this desert environment. Here are a few tips and suggestions to assist in making your family visit safe and enjoyable:

• Children of all ages should be taught about the dangers in the desert. Cacti are probably the most commonly encountered danger. The yucca, with its deadly spears oftentimes right at eye level of the little ones, should be given a wide berth.

• Children should also be warned to always be on the lookout for snakes. Rattlesnakes blend into the environment very well, and kids tend to crawl and explore in the very nooks and crannies that they like to hide in. Snakes avoid people and so they are less likely to be found in areas that are frequented by people. I like to case out the area for rattlesnakes before letting my three-year-old daughter loose.

• Consider walking one of the large official trails; they tend to be safer in general. Here are a suggested few: Hidden Valley Loop Trail, Barker Dam Trail, Cap Rock Loop Trail, Skull Rock Trail.

• Several picnic areas can be found in the Park. These spots have picnic tables, restrooms, parking, and even barbeques, making for an excellent place where families can set up a day-camp and hang out. Picnic sites can be found at: Quail Springs, Hidden Valley, Cap Rock, Live Oak, Split Rock, Rattlesnake Canyon, and Lower Covington Flats.

• Children should wear sunscreen, even in winter months and overcast skies, as the sun is insense and there is little shade to be found.

• Children should be encouraged to drink plenty of liquids, and often. Remember that adults can require up to a gallon of water per day in the hot months, so little ones also need plenty of hydration.

Technical difficulty: This 1-5 rating considers the unique difficulties of the terrain. Many hikes in Joshua Tree involve such challenges as deep-sand hiking, climbing over or squeezing under boulders, or scaling a steep embankment with loose rock. A rating of 1 means walking on a flat, well-worn trail. A rating of 5 might indicate extended rock scrambling with difficult sections, or ascending a steep rock face with risk of fall and injury.

Navigating: A 1-5 rating of how difficult it is to stay on course. Some trails are easily followed; others can be difficult to see. Other hikes have no trail, but only a distant landmark on the horizon to guide the way. A rating of 1 would be well-worn trail with signage. A rating of 5 might indicate a hike that includes extensive cross-country, off-trail travel with few landmarks.

A climber reaches for a "thank god hold" while ascending the North Astrodome, one of the largest chunks of rock in the Park, located deep in the Wonderland of Rocks.

Trail type: This notes the type of path encountered on the hike. Official trails are usually well-worn, well-marked with signs, and are the easiest of all trail types to follow. Climber trails are often well-worn and sometimes even marked with signs. Game trails are small and sometimes hard to follow. "Cross-country" means that there are no trails, just land features to follow. Other trail types listed are self explanatory.

ROCK CLIMBING

Joshua Tree National Park is widely regarded as one of the top destinations in the world for rock climbing. On any given day, hundreds of climbers can be found scaling the many granite domes and boulders throughout the Mojave side of the park. It is said that there are over 8000 individual climbing routes, located on 600 different cliffs and formations. The history of rock climbing in Joshua Tree goes back to the mid-1940s. Many of the original bolts and pitons from that time, still affixed to the cliffs, are now considered cultural artifacts by the National Park Service and are protected by law.

Rock climbing is a dangerous sport, and should never be attempted without proper instruction. Several rock-climbing guide services operate within the Park, offering regular classes. This is probably the best way to learn, hands-on, what the sport is really about. For more information on rock climbing, see Rock Climbing 101 on page 77. For experienced climbers, guidebooks are available at the visitors centers, or at one of several climbing stores at the corner of Highway 62 and Park Boulevard in the town of Joshua Tree, or at www.wolverinepublishing.com.

BIKING

Bicycles are restricted to public access roads only. For those who like to ride pavement, Joshua Tree is an amazing place. Roads lead through just about every area of the Park. The stretch of Park Boulevard between the West Entrance and Intersection Rock seems to be the most popular ride. Keys View Road is also a nice ride. Unfortunately, there are no bike lanes in the Park, so use caution!

Mountain Biking: Very few options exist for those who like to get off of the pavement. Bikes are strictly prohibited from being ridden on anything other than public access roads. Riding on trails is prohibited. There are dirt roads that are OK to ride on, many of them leading into less-traveled areas of the Park. For those seeking challenging terrain, there is really only one option — the end of Old Dale Road. The end of Old Dale Road rises steeply into the Pinto Mountains, quickly becoming rocky and rutted on its way into the rugged mountains. After several miles the road exits the Park's boundaries, where off-road riding is acceptable. Be advised that the first 10 miles of Old Dale Road has long stretches of deep sand, so riders may want to drive this initial section. Also be advised that this is a remote section of the Park. Encountering others is rare; entering this area in the hotter months is not recommended.

HORSEBACK RIDING

For those who own horses, Joshua Tree is a unique and beautiful place to ride. The Park offers over 250 miles of equestrian trails and corridors (some are still in development), many of which penetrate deep into the backcountry of the Park. Horse-accommodating campsites and parking lots can be found, usually located strategically near equestrian trails.

Stock use is limited to horses and mules. Riding is limited to equestrian trails, designated corridors, public-accessible dirt roads, and the shoulders of paved roads. Riders can enter the Park on horseback at Black Rock, the West Entrance, the Burro Loop, and the North Entrance. Equestrian parking and staging areas can be found at: The Boy Scout Trailhead, Indian Cove, Lower Covington Flats Picnic Area, the West Entrance Borrow Pit, Twin Tanks Backcountry Board and parking lot, Geology Tour Road Backcountry Board and parking lot, the North Entrance, Black Rock Backcountry Board and parking lot, and Ryan Campground. Trailers may also be parked at other locations as long as they do not obstruct traffic.

Both Ryan Campground and Black Rock Campground have horse-accommodating campsites (Ryan: $10 per night, Black Rock: $15

per night). Water is available at Black Rock, but not at Ryan. Reservations can be made for horse camps at Black Rock and Ryan Campgrounds, but are not required. Backcountry camping with horses is also allowed, but by permit only. A few other rules that apply:

• Riders should travel single file to reduce impact.

• Stock animals are not permitted within ¼ mile of any natural or constructed water source. Riders must bring their own water for stock.

• Grazing is not permitted in the Park. Stock animals are restricted to pellet feed.

• Manure must be removed from campgrounds, parking lots, and trailheads.

OFF-ROADING

Motorized vehicles are ONLY permitted on established roads inside of Joshua Tree National Park. There are, however, several old mine roads open to vehicular traffic that are quite rugged and lead to off-road areas located just outside of Park boundaries. This book covers three of these roads: Little Berdoo Canyon Road, Old Dale Road, and Pinkham Canyon Road. This is by no means a comprehensive list.

• Little Berdoo Canyon Road: This road descends a deep, sandy canyon with a small amount of rock crawling. It eventually leads to Coachella Valley. The road can be found at the end of Geology Tour Road in Chapter 5. See page 149 for more details.

• Old Dale Road: This road follows a historical teamsters route through a major mining district, ascending steep, rocky hills on its deeply rutted course. The road exits at Highway 62, about 10 miles east of the town of 29 Palms. See Chapter 7, page 197, for more details.

• Pinkham Canyon Road: This route travels a washboard road across the open plains of the Cottonwood area before ducking into a deep canyon and descending to Interstate 10. See Chapter 8, page 210, for more details.

"Where Eagles Dare": Looking into the interior of Joshua Tree from Covington Flats. The view includes the Quail Springs area, the Wonderland of Rocks, and Queen Mountain, the peak at the center.

JOSHUA TREE NATIONAL PARK HISTORY

In 1994, Congress passed the Desert Protections Act, transferring three million acres of prime American desert into the care of the National Park Service (NPS). This land transfer added 234,000 acres to Joshua Tree National Monument, elevating it to National Park status. Since that time, the NPS has transformed a dusty little desert oddity into a world attraction.

Man's fascination with this peculiar place goes back many thousands of years. Long before Columbus and the civilized world "discovered" America, even before the Polynesians began their epic crossing of the Pacific, there was Pinto Man, believed to have migrated into the Americas during a past Ice Age. Pinto culture artifacts found in Joshua Tree have been dated from 4,000 years up to 9,000 years in age. The land that these peoples lived on was much different than what we see here today, with verdant canyons, grassy plains, and flowing rivers. Pinto Basin, in the lower Sonoran portion of Joshua Tree, was one such place. Within it, an ancient culture lived for untold generations, before quietly disappearing. At some later date, native Serrano, Cahuilla, and Chemehuevi Indians moved into the high plains of Joshua Tree. Equipped with a deep understanding of desert life, they thrived on the cornucopia of resources that this arid paradise offered. Their symbiotic way of life remained unchanged for eons, until one fateful morning in the mid-1800s, when a wily old prospector by the name of John "Quartz" Wilson wandered through the area looking for a shortcut to San Bernardino. He stumbled upon a boulder laced with "color," forever changing the face of paradise. Gold fever! Turn-of-the-century industrialism, cattle rustling, racketeering, fraud, shootouts, murder — the tales spin like a cheap dime-store novel. The Wild West fully embraced Joshua Tree, as the many impromptu graves scattered throughout the Park will attest, but by the late 1920s, most of the big operations had played out. The bustle of teamsters wagons and shantytowns were gone, and the shootouts and horseback gangs faded into the history books.

It was around this time that Joshua Tree was first seen as a destination for recreation. By the close of the 1920s, when America was experiencing the auto revolution, Los Angelinos began touring outside the city, eventually finding the old teamster's routes that led into what is now Joshua Tree. The area quickly gained a reputation for being a strange and beautiful place to visit, drawing curious city dwellers in increasing numbers. This newfound appreciation of the desert came with a price, though, as many visitors took home cactus and other "souvenirs" of the desert, slowly and unintentionally changing the land. Another disturbing trend was that of setting Joshua trees on fire at night as "nightlights." This genocide of the local flora caught the eye of one local member of high society, Minerva Hoyt. An unlikely champion of the desert, the affluent Mrs. Hoyt fought long and seemingly impossible battles, taking on big, unionized mining companies and pro-development government policies, not to mention the public's general attitude that the desert was a barren and worthless place. Mrs. Hoyt persevered, and on August 10, 1936, President Roosevelt signed a proclamation that set aside 825,000 acres of California high desert as Joshua Tree National Monument.

The publicity received from the newly formed Monument brought in a new wave of auto-touring clubs and other organizations, including the Sierra Club. Joshua Tree was finally being appreciated for its beauty and not for its material value. The Monument's status suffered a setback in the 1950s, when legislation, under extreme pressure from special-interest mining organizations, transferred 289,000 acres back into public domain, opening it back up to mining. Today, Joshua Tree National Park covers about 780,000 acres and enjoys the full protection afforded by National Park status.

GEOLOGY OF JOSHUA TREE

Driving through Joshua Tree National Park, one cannot help but ponder the geological forces that shaped this wondrous place. Located just miles from the mighty San Andreas Fault, and sitting on the cusp of the North American Tectonic Plate, the ancient landscape tells tales of incomprehensible forces and of inconceivable timescales.

Ultimately, the processes that shaped the Park can be traced back billions of years, but for the juicy bits we need only go back a scant 280 million. The land we see as Joshua Tree National Park was born when the Pacific Plate began to slip beneath the North American Plate. This process, known as subduction, was responsible for uplifting the Colorado Plateau, creating the Rocky Mountains, and also lifting California from beneath the ocean floor.

As the Pacific Plate continued to slide beneath the North American Plate, friction from the two plates created extreme heat, melting the overlying mantel wedge and creating huge bubbles of magma. These magma bubbles, known as plutons, cooled to become the granite of Joshua Tree (and much of the granite in California). Subduction continued on and off until about 25 million years ago, when an enormous chunk of the Pacific Plate broke off, sinking deep into the earth. At this time, the plate boundary transformed from a subduction fault to a lateral-slip fault—the San Andreas Fault was born!

The San Andreas Fault is actually a system of faults that run some 800 miles through California. Just south of Joshua Tree National Park, the fault negotiates a large spur in the North

Patchy clouds accentuate the rugged high country of Joshua Tree National Park in this 100-mile view from the Ryan Mountain trail. The sea of rock at midphoto is the Wonderland of Rocks.

American Plate. This area of the fault is known as the "Big Bend." Immense pressure from the two plates hooking up at the spur has shattered the region into many faults and blocks. These "fault blocks" move independently from each other; some rotate, some drop down, others lift and even tilt. The "high plateau" of Joshua Tree is actually a group of uplifted fault blocks. The Big Bend in the San Andreas Fault is also responsible for the unusual Transverse Mountain Ranges of Southern California, of which Joshua Tree forms the eastern terminus.

      The most common rock in the Park is called White Tank Monzogranite. This is the coarse, tan-colored rock typically seen as large domes or piles of boulders. The forces that sculpted these formations, called Inselbergs, began deep within the earth's crust. Back track a bit to the plutons we discussed earlier. The plutons are thought to have formed up to 10 miles below the surface. High pressure and slow cooling crystallized the magma into the coarse monzogranite of the Park. After millions of years of erosion and uplift, the granitic plutons finally neared the surface. Relieved of the overlying pressures, joints (cracks) formed in the now-solid rock. As a result of being freed from the weight above, the granite began shelling off thin layers, similar to the skin of an onion. When the granite finally surfaced it was already extensively fragmented. Chemical reactions with water attacked the rock, rounding off the fragments into boulders of all shapes and sizes, and welling out hollows (called tafoni). Finally, erosion removed the loose debris and soil from between the boulders, as they slowly settled into the characteristic rock piles that now define the Joshua Tree landscape.

Deep in the Wonderland of Rocks, a mature male Bighorn Sheep stands his ground against a slightly intimidated photographer.

WILDLIFE

Take a stroll into the wilds of Joshua Tree and you may get the impression that nothing at all exists out here, save for lizards and an occasional bird. This of course is not the case. The Park supports a wide variety of mammals, birds, reptiles, insects, and even a few amphibians. Due to extreme daytime temperatures, many desert creatures have adopted nocturnal habits. Of the species that do brave the sun, camouflage often renders them difficult to spot. Birds and lizards are the exception; they can usually be sighted everywhere in the Park.

Mammals – 52 species of mammal exist within Joshua Tree's boundaries. Many of these are varieties of rodents (24) and bats (12). Several species of larger mammals live within the Park. Coyotes are common, and their yips and howls can usually be heard throughout the night. They also occasionally skulk around on the road and near picnic areas, looking for handouts. (Please do not feed them! Not only is it illegal, but habituated beggars may be euthanized.) Bobcats and mountain lions exist in the Park, but they are exceedingly rare. Bighorn sheep, a threatened species, are fairly common in the Park. Many visitors are treated to bighorn sightings, especially along the perimeters of

A female Leopard Lizard donning mating colors, Indian Cove.

A large flock of quail get in some last minute foraging just as a powerful winter storm begins to unleash its payload.

the Wonderland. Black-tail deer have been known to inhabit the higher elevations of Joshua Tree. Other creatures include ringtail cats, cottontail and jack rabbits, the common gray fox, and the very uncommon kit fox.

Birds – Over 250 species of bird have been spotted in the Park, which is considered an excellent place for birdwatching. Many of these species are migratory travelers, as the Park lies within a major migration corridor called the Pacific Flyway. Some of the more exotic migrants include: Scotts Oriole, Hooded Oriole, Western Tanager, Scarlet Tanager, American Robin, Western Bluebird, Cedar Waxwing, and Golden Eagle. Spring and fall are the best times to look for these migrants. 78 bird species are permanent residents. Raven, Gambel's Quail, Roadrunner, Mockingbird, Blue Jay, Cactus Wren, Burrowing Owls, Great Horned Owls, Anna's Hummingbird, and Mourning Dove are some of the birds that call Joshua Tree their year-round home.

This old Desert Tortoise has probably been around longer than most of us!

Reptiles – Think of a desert creature and the first thing that comes to mind is a reptile, usually a snake or a lizard. Joshua Tree is no exception, with 18 species of lizard and 25 species of snake found within its boundaries. The Park is also home to the endangered Desert Tortoise. Lizard species include: Banded Gecko, Desert Iguana, Collard Lizard, Leopard Lizard, Chuckwalla, Horned Lizard, Whiptail, Desert Skink, and the Silvery Legless Lizard. Snake species are even more prolific, with varieties such as: Desert Blind Snake, California King Snake, Rosy Boa, Coachwhip, Striped Racer, Leaf-Nosed Snake, and Gopher Snake, not to mention seven venomous pit vipers including the Western Diamondback, Mojave Sidewinder, Colorado Sidewinder, Speckled Rattlesnake, Red Diamond Rattlesnake, Mojave Rattlesnake, and the most lethal of them all, the Southern Pacific Rattlesnake!

Amphibians – Believe it or not, Joshua Tree National Park is home to two species of amphibian: The California Tree Frog and the Red Spotted Toad. Both species spend much of their lives underground or in subterranean crevices, where they wait for the heavy rains of late summer. After a heavy shower they come out in quantities, mate, and then retreat to their moist dens.

A feisty tarantula guards her den near White Tank Campground.

Insects, Arachnids, and other Creepy Crawlies

As with every other crevice and corner of the world, Joshua Tree has its share of insects, bugs, and creepy crawlies. The most common critters found in the Park within this genre are probably ants and Stink Beetles; the latter being those shiny black bugs that poke their butts up in the air if you mess with them. The Park has several varieties of ant. Harvester ants make a large mound at the entrance to their nest, sometimes 2 or 3 feet in diameter, composed mostly of discarded bits of plants that they collect and store in their underground caverns. Harvester ant trails can be up to a foot wide, with many thousands of ants shuffling along. Tarantulas exist in the Park, and are somewhat common on the eastern "Colorado Desert" side, especially in the late summer when they come out to mate. Tarantula Hawks are also common. Tarantula Hawks are large (2- to 3-inch long) black wasps with bright orange wings. The sight of them has a way of inciting a primal terror in most humans. (Not to worry, though: they are looking for spiders, not people, and are unlikely to attack unless antagonized.) Several species of scorpion are known to exist in the Park, but sightings are rare. Giant six-inch-long black millipedes can sometimes be spotted in the wee hours. The Park has over 75 varieties of butterfly, from the large and stunning Tiger Swallowtail to the tiny Western Pygmy Blue, one of the smallest butterflies in the world. Several varieties of dragonfly and damselfly can also be seen darting around, including Flame Skipper, Green Darner, and the Blue Dasher.

A bobcat sunning on a cold winter morning in Hidden Valley.

CALIFORNIA RIDING AND HIKING TRAIL

The California Riding and Hiking Trail is an epic 35-mile journey, crossing the entire Mojave high-desert portion of Joshua Tree National Park. Multi-day backpacking is beyond the scope of this book, but this trail is worth mentioning due to its significance in the Park's trail system. As its name suggests, the trail is open to both equestrian use and hiking. To complete its entire length on foot typically takes two to three days. Most start at Black Rock Campground, where the terrain gradually descends to its low point at the North Entrance. The trail is well maintained, has signs along the way, and is generally easy to follow.

The trail is broken into five sections, each being a stretch between major roads. All five sections are worthy trails on their own, complete with large parking lots and Backcountry Boards at each intersection. See overview map on page 32.

Section 1: Black Rock to Covington Flats
Distance: 7.6 miles one-way
See maps on pages 215 and 222

The start is at the entrance to Black Rock Backcountry Board and parking lot; the finish is at Upper Covington Flats parking. Take the obvious trail east, joining with a wash for a bit before exiting on the left. The trail rises onto a hillside, with some nice vistas of Yucca Valley and the deserts to the north. The trail will eventually drop down into a system of washes. Signs mark the proper path in this area. Continue uphill in the wash, which will become a tight canyon, bending to the south. Eventually the trail will drop down out of the mountainous country and onto the flats, crossing through a burn area that makes an eerie contrast to the piñon pine forests behind. Continuing south, the trail will eventually parallel the Upper Covington Flats Road before reaching the parking lot at Upper Covington Flats.

Section 2: Upper Covington Flats to Keys View Road
Distance: 11.3 miles one-way
See maps on pages 222 and 115

The start is at Upper Covington Flats Backcountry Board and parking lot; the finish is at Juniper Flats Backcountry Board. Take the obvious trail behind the board, heading east. The trail passes below some huge Joshua trees before heading into steep hills. Dropping down out of the steep hills on the other side, the trail travels out into Lower Juniper Flats. From here, the trail travels southeast to the furthest corner of Lower Juniper Flats before rising onto a plateau and continuing along a ridge. From the ridge, excellent views of Coachella Valley and the Salton Sea can be enjoyed. Next, the trail negotiates a series of rugged canyons and washes, eventually rising back onto the Juniper Flats plateau. The final 4 miles travels flat ground, through dense forests of junipers and Joshua trees. Juniper Flats Backcountry Board and parking lot marks the end of this section of the trail. (It is possible however, to cross the road and finish at Ryan Campground, 0.7 miles further.)

Section 3: Keys Road to Geology Tour Road
Distance: 6.5 miles one-way
See maps on pages 115 and 132

The start is at Juniper Flats Backcountry Board and parking lot (or Ryan Campground); the finish is at Geology Tour Road Backcountry Board. Walk the spur trail on the right side (NE corner) of the parking lot, heading north for 100 yards to join the main CRHT. Turn right and follow the trail, crossing the road, and then on to Ryan Campground some 0.7 miles away. Veer right at the campground, now heading east. The trail will wander through a Joshua tree forest, then head through a gap in the hills. From there, the trail winds down through rugged hills, ending up on the desert floor of Queen Valley. Several old mining prospects can be found here. (An old legend tells of a Spanish mine here that is haunted.) From the valley floor, the trail bends to the left, heading northeast on a gentle incline toward Geology Tour Road, some 3.3 miles distant.

Section 4: Geology Tour Road to Pinto Basin Road
Distance: 4.3 miles one-way
See maps on pages 132 and 161

The start is at the Geology Tour Road Backcountry Board and parking lot; the finish is at the Twin Tanks Backcountry Board on Pinto Basin Road near White Tank Campground. This is the easiest of the five sections of the CRHT, since travel is almost entirely downhill. This section starts out by traveling east across the open desert. The trail slowly veers to the southeast, passing near some rock piles after about 1.5 miles. From there, the trail descends into a lower valley, veering to the left and heading northeast for the remainder. This portion of the hike offers expansive views of the wide-open desert, Stirrup Tank canyon, and the rugged Hexie Mountains beyond. The section ends at the Twin Tanks Backcountry Board and parking lot, which is actually 250 yards north of where the CHRT crosses over Pinto Basin Road. A short spur trail connects the two.

Section 5: Pinto Basin Road to the North Entrance
Distance: 7.5 miles one-way
See map on page 161

The start is at Twin Tanks Backcountry Board and parking lot; the finish is at the North Entrance. From the parking lot, travel south for 250 yards on a spur trail leading to the CRHT. Join that trail and turn left (NE), crossing Pinto Basin Road and shortly thereafter veering to the north. The trail skirts along the edge of large boulder fields as it travels to a highpoint, then begins its gradual descent, ultimately to the boundary of the Park. At mile 2.5, the trail crosses over a paved service road, then turns right, traveling around a large hill. Past the hill, the trail continues downhill, where the valley opens up to reveal the massive alluvial slope leading to 29 Palms. Rugged mountain ranges line the valley. After 3.2 miles, the trail will bend to the left, traveling northwest for just over a mile to the North Entrance station.

Photo opposite: Intergalactic harmony: Late-summer Milky Way
display over a giant Joshua tree in Lost Horse Valley.

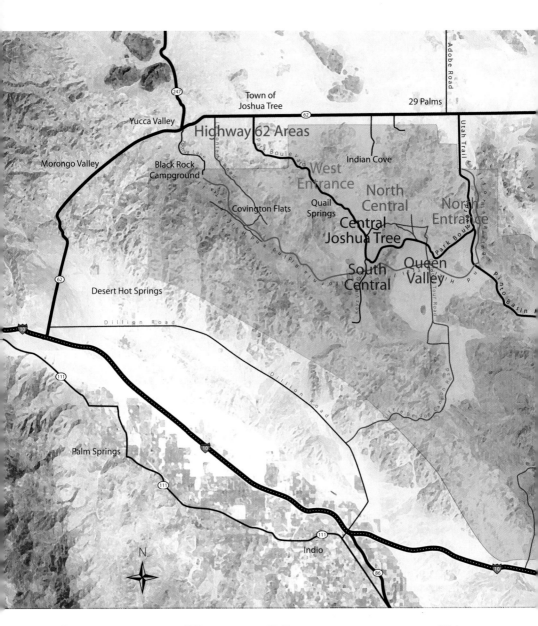

JOSHUA TREE NATIONAL PARK

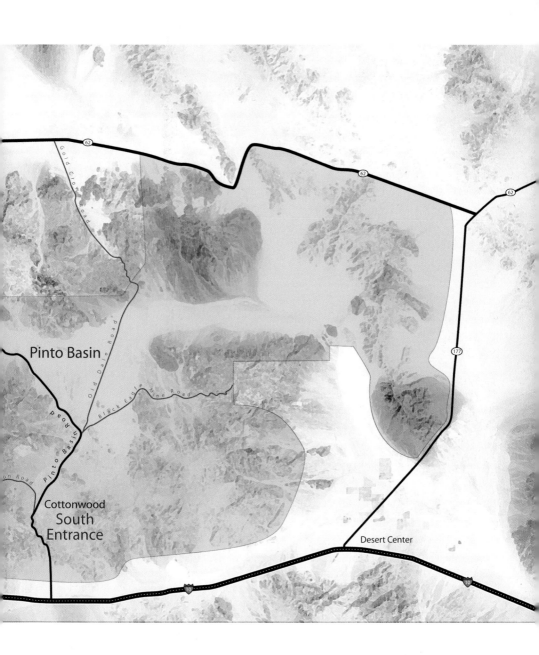

Pinto Basin

Cottonwood
South
Entrance

Desert Center

CHAPTER 1
THE WEST ENTRANCE

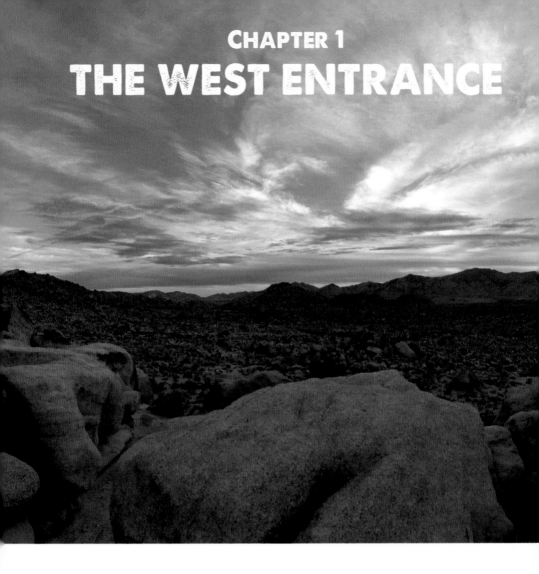

Welcome to Joshua Tree National Park! This chapter begins about 5 miles before the Park's West Entrance, at the West Entrance Visitors Center. It's a good place to start for those wanting to obtain information on the Park, make reservations for campgrounds, or to sign up for guided tours. From the visitors center, Park Boulevard winds its way through the community of Monument Manor to the West Entrance, 5 miles distant. At busy times—usually 10 AM to noon on peak-season weekends—there may be a line of cars waiting to enter at the West Entrance kiosk. Restrooms and water can be found here.

Once inside the Park, the road gently rises as it travels southeast, winding into the high country. Visitors should keep a vigilant eye out for the endangered Desert Tortoise, which has been known to cross the road in this part of the Park. At 1.8 miles from the entrance is the first hike, the North View Trail. This trail leads to a high lookout with views of Yucca Valley, the town of Joshua Tree, and Lucerne Valley beyond. The trail traverses a maze of gullies and ridges and can be difficult to follow.

A balanced rock points like a compass needle toward the interior of the Park. Photographed near the North View Trail.

At 2.5 miles from the entrance, the curious visitor will encounter a large turnout with an informational plaque and a small trail leading off into the nearby hills. It's a good place to get out of the car and stretch. As you continue east, the landscape opens up into the high desert of Joshua Tree National Park. At approximately 3.5 miles, the road passes between the first (of many!) real rock piles on the journey. Several small pullouts dot this area, and there is also a large paved turnout 1/4 mile further. A small trail leads to the summit of the rocky knoll on the right (S), and just beyond, a faint mine road leads to one of the all-time secrets of Joshua Tree: Samuelson's Rocks.

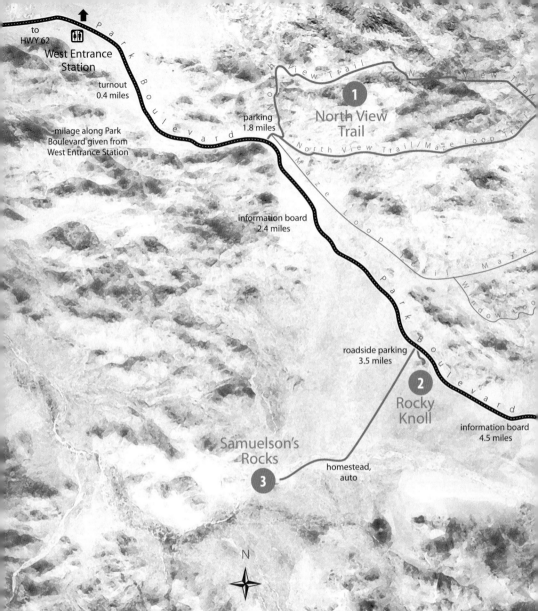

to
HWY 62

West Entrance
Station

turnout
0.4 miles

milage along Park
Boulevard given from
West Entrance Station

Park Boulevard

parking
1.8 miles

information board
2.4 miles

North View Trail

North View Trail

North View Trail

1

North View
Trail

North View Trail/Maze Loop Trail

Maze Loop Trail

Park Boulevard

Maze

Window loop

roadside parking
3.5 miles

2

Rocky
Knoll

information board
4.5 miles

Samuelson's
Rocks

3

homestead,
auto

N

THE WEST
ENTRANCE

to
Indian Cove

Willow Hole   **4**

Wagmarken
Hill

1

rnout
iles

Backcountry Board

Wonderland North
parking lot 6.2 miles

parking
5.8 miles

"Keys Corner"

Quail Springs
Picnic Area

Keys Ranch

Central Joshua
Tree North
(Chapter 3)

parking
7.4 miles

Central
Joshua Tree
(Chapter 2)

Echo Rock

Hidden Valley
Campground

Top: Rocks with views to the northwest, near the beginning of the North View Trail. Middle: Sights along the trail.

HIKE

North View Trail - #1

Total distance: 4.7 miles (loop)
Physical difficulty: 3
Technical difficulty: 2
Navigating: 2
Trail type: official trail

The North View Trail traverses some truly beautiful Joshua Tree country, traveling through the mountains and craggy peaks that form the northern edge of the Park's high plateau. There are amazing vistas to be taken in around every corner on the first half of this trek. The second half of the journey drops down out of the hills and into a maze of washes, where tall nolinas can be found drooping over the trail, dwarf junipers grow out of the sides of rock outcroppings, and eroded rocks assume a myriad of shapes and forms. This moderately strenuous trail starts out traveling north across rolling hills towards the edge of the Joshua Tree plateau. The hills gradually become more rugged as the trail forges on, seemingly wandering all over the place between craggy peaks and deep ravines on its way to a high ridge. The walk along the ridge offers spectacular views of the low-desert to the north. Just past the ridge, a large piñon pine can be found growing out of a jumble of flat rocks, which makes a perfect rest stop. From there, the trail drops down into the deep washes known as The Maze, where it meets up with the Maze Loop Trail. At this point hikers can decide to either travel the shorter North Maze Access (4.7 miles), or the longer South Maze Access (5.8 miles) back to the parking lot. Note that there is another extension off of the South Maze Access, known as the Windows Loop; see map for details.

Details: Park at a dirt turnout on the north side of Park Boulevard, located 1.8 miles east of the West Entrance station. Take the trail heading northeast for 100 yards to a sandy

Top: Looking northeast toward the 29 Palms Marine Base on the North View Trail. Bottom: Delicate Window, North View Trail.

wash (signs along the way note several other trails that also start from this location). Turn right (SE) and travel 100 yards up the wash to another sign noting the Maze Loop north access to the right, and the North View Trail to the left. Take the left trail, which immediately climbs a hill, bending to the left and traveling north across rolling hills with occasional wash crossings. At 0.6 miles, the trail will enter an alcove with rocky peaks and cliffs where there is an excellent view of Lucerne Valley and the desert to the northwest. The trail will circle this alcove and then exit up a steep hillside, now heading southeast. Once over the hill, the trail drops down into a prominent drainage, following it (E) back uphill to a saddle between two tall peaks. A sign here denotes a short side trail leading to a good viewpoint of Copper Mountain. Continue on the main trail as it trends to the right (SE), uphill to a flat behind the tallest peak in the area. Once on the flat, there's another sign denoting a side trail to the West Hills Viewpoint. From here, the trail turns left (E), traveling along a high ridge with 100-mile views across the low deserts of Southern California, before dropping down into a valley, where the excellent pine tree rest stop is found. Past the tree, the trail heads over one last hill before dropping down into a

deep sandy wash. Follow the wash that winds its way to the east (keep an eye out for signs that mark the trail in tricky spots). Eventually, the trail will bend to the right (S) to a junction, with a sign noting the Big Pine Trail to the left (E), and the Maze Connection to the right (SW). Head to the right, following a shallow wash for another 0.2 miles, to a second junction with the Maze Trail. If you're up for more adventure, take the left "south access" trail (4 miles to parking lot), which winds through additional rocky hills. Otherwise, take the right "north access" trail (1.6 miles to parking lot), which leads gently uphill (W) through a sandy wash for 0.25 miles, and then gently downhill for the remainder of the hike via shallow washes with rocky borders.

Looking east into central Joshua Tree from the vicinity of the Rocky Knoll. The islands of rocks are called inselbergs in geology lingo.

HIKE

Rocky Knoll - #2

Total distance: 0.25 miles (round trip)
Physical difficulty: 2
Technical difficulty: 3
Navigating: 1
Trail type: undeveloped path

This short jaunt leads straight up a rock formation close to the road. There is no official trail here, but ascending the hill has become so popular that a small trail has formed on its northwest flank. The path is steep, so a bit of "hands-on" rock scrambling is required to reach the summit plateau. Once near the summit, an enclosed flat area can be found with nice views of the surrounding terrain. A dramatic pinnacle can be gained with a bit more scrambling.

Details: Park Boulevard weaves between several rock piles, and then the Rocky Knoll comes into view on the road's south side. Park at dirt turnouts approximately 3.5 miles from the West Entrance. Please DO NOT pull straight into the desert; past problems have caused the Park Service to consider removing the pullouts altogether! There are several trails that lead up the rock pile, all of which converge higher up the hill before trending into a gully. Some rock scrambling is encountered at the top of the gully just before reaching the flat area. To continue on to the true summit, rock hop straight toward it, then turn right (W) and scramble up the ridge.

HIKE

Samuelson's Rocks - #3

Total distance: 2.8 miles (round trip)
Physical difficulty: 1
Technical difficulty: 1
Navigating: 2
Trail type: cross-country/no trail

Something about the desert changes a person over time—maybe it's the heat or the dry air. Some say it's an awakening; others call it madness! For John Samuelson, that epiphany manifested as a series of strange sayings meticulously etched into the rocks around the hill at what was then his homestead. Most of the etchings make little to no sense, and the grammar is rife with mistakes—perfectly quirky for this odd realm called Joshua Tree!

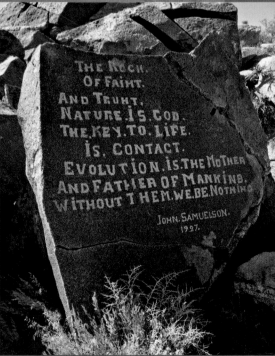

Details: One of the all-time local secrets of Joshua Tree! Locals will no doubt be hunting me down with pitchforks and forget-me-sticks for letting loose this little chestnut. From turnouts at 3.5 miles, walk SSW into the open desert, traveling to the right of Rocky Knoll. There is a faint mine road, but it can be hard to see at times. Follow the mine road gently downhill for about 1/2 mile. At about the middle of the valley is a large wash traveling east/west;

follow it to the right (W). Close to this point is a collapsed structure with the remains of an old auto. Continue down the wash for another 1/2 mile to where it meets a rocky hill. Samuelson's Rocks are strewn around this hill, along with a spring bed and other weird stuff. Around the back of the hill are a corral and water tank. Keep in mind that everything found here is protected by law and should not be disturbed or removed.

Old truck near Samuelson's Rocks. Inset: Samuelson etchings.

Vagmarken Hill photographed at night.

VAGMARKEN HILL

Once past the Rocky Knoll area, the view opens up to reveal the heart and soul of Joshua Tree—millions upon millions of granite boulders and rock piles interlaced with Joshua tree forests so thick they look like grass. At mile 4.75 is a large dirt turnout with an informational plaque describing a wildfire that swept through this area several decades ago. Across the road from the turnout is the large, rocky Vagmarken Hill. Hiking to its summit is technically quite easy, but very steep for about 400 feet of vertical relief. It's possible to ascend either side, but the west end is a bit easier. The summit has a large flat area with faint signs of mining activity.

QUAIL SPRINGS PICNIC AREA

Quail Spring Picnic Area.

Continuing east along Park Boulevard, the next point of interest is the Quail Springs Picnic Area at 5.8 miles. This stop consists of picnic tables, restrooms, and a few barbeques scattered around the base of a squat granite monolith. Kids and grown-ups alike will enjoy crawling over and under the many boulders piled up here, and the main rock formation is an easy scramble to reach its summit. Travelers may also get their first glimpse of rock climbers, as the largest rock (affectionately known as Trashcan Rock) is a popular spot. Several long trails branch off from the rear parking lot. One leads to the nearby hills approximately 3/4 mile to the west; the other travels NE on a faint dirt road that used to be the old Quail Springs Road. The old road eventually branches to the left and into a deep canyon that leads to Johnny Lang's abandoned mine and homestead. (It's approximately 4 miles to the mine.) Continuing on the old Quail Springs Road will eventually lead to the Samuelson's Rocks area.

"Stones of chance," in the north part of the Wonderland.

The Boy Scout Trail leading off toward the granite labyrinth of the Wonderland North.

HIKE

Willow Hole Trail - #4

Hiking into Willow Hole.

Total distance: 7 miles round trip
Physical difficulty: 3
Technical difficulty: 1
Navigating: 3
Trail type: official trail, wash

The Wonderland of Rock is truly a wonder of the world. Countless rocks of every conceivable shape and size lie piled up in this corner of the park. Only the most experienced of Joshua Tree wanderers should explore its more intricate labyrinths, but there are a few prominent canyons that forge deeply into the heart of the Wonderland that take much of the guesswork out of navigating the massive maze of monzonite. This adventure travels through several of these large canyons, leading to a beautiful spring on the edge of the northern plateau of Joshua Tree. The trail first heads out into open desert, passing random rock piles before following the edge of towering walls of granite boulders. Then, almost as if to escape, the trail ducks into the maze of rocks. Before long, wanderers will find themselves in deep canyons with massive piles of granite towering overhead. Eventually

the sandy washes meet the northern edge of the Joshua Tree plateau, and the whole rocky landscape drops away into Indian Cove thousands of feet below. The "Hole," located at this edge, is a dense thicket of willow trees, and often times there is also a watery mire. This is a prime location for observing wildlife.

Details: Find the large Wonderland of Rocks North parking lot 6.5 miles east of the West Entrance. Restrooms and a Backcountry Board can be found here. The primary trail here is the Boy Scout Trail, a 7.5-mile, one-way excursion to Indian Cove (see next page). The Willow Hole Trail follows the Boy Scout Trail for 1.25 miles before branching off. Starting at the Backcountry Board in the parking lot, take the Boy Scout Trail north across the open desert. After 1 mile, veer left (N) at a junction and walk to a second junction with a sign. The left fork is the continuation of the Boy Scout Trail

and the right trail leads to Willow Hole. Take the right trail and walk for another mile as the trail bends to the right (E). Soon the trail heads into the rocks alongside a large sandy wash, and after several hundred yards both the trail and the wash bend sharply to the right (S). Continue, heading south, as the trail and the wash join. After another couple hundred yards, the wash will bend sharply to the left (E). Follow the wash east to a junction with deep sand. Take the left junction, ducking between some large boulders into an adjacent wash. This wash will curve back around and then straighten out, heading north. Continue in the deep, sandy wash as it eventually bends right (E) and then leads directly into Willow Hole. To return, retrace your steps.

Although beyond the scope of this book, an adventurous link-up into Rattlesnake Canyon (page 228) is possible, traveling steeply downhill from behind Willow Hole.

BOY SCOUT HIKING AND EQUESTRIAN TRAIL:

The Boy Scout Trail is an 8-mile, one-way trek leading from the interior of the Park down into the low desert at the far north side. Often done as a two-day backpack trip, it's longer than most of the hikes covered in this book. It is worth mentioning, though, as it is a fine hike, also open to equestrian use. The trail is most commonly done "downhill," south to north, starting at Wonderland North and finishing at Indian Cove.

The trail starts out with a long stroll across the open plains of Joshua Tree, traveling through forests of Joshua trees and the occasional rock pile. Excellent backcountry camping can be found along this section of the trail. At the far north end of the open plain, the trail enters a maze of rocky hills, eventually dropping down into a deep canyon wash that leads to the low desert floor at Indian Cove. At the bottom of the canyon, the drainage opens up into a huge sandy wash. From there, the trail roams across creosote desert to the northern terminus of the trail.

DETAILS: This description is from south to north, starting at the Wonderland North parking lot and ending at the Boy Scout parking lot in Indian Cove. The Wonderland of Rocks North parking lot is located off Park Boulevard, 6.5 miles east of the West Entrance. Restrooms and a Backcountry Board can be found here. From the Backcountry Board, travel north on the large trail. At mile 1, the trail will bend left at a barely visible old road, and then bend left again 0.25 miles further. A junction with a sign notes the Willow Hole Trail to the right, and the Boy Scout Trail to the left. Take the left fork and continue on. At 3.8 miles the trail will drop into a sandy wash, following it north for 0.6 miles before exiting on the left side, where it crosses over a saddle and then drops down steeply into a large canyon and wash. The trail follows alongside this wash. After several hundred yards, the canyon will bend to the right (E) where the trail then enters the wash, fording deep sand for the next mile. At 5.7 miles the trail exits the wash on its right side, climbing a knoll, and then dropping back down into the wash, which has now opened up on the desert floor. Continue in the wash for 300 yards to where the trail exits on the right side (E), heading across the open desert for a final 1.5 miles to the parking lot.

Piñon pine snag and rock formation, Wonderland North.

Stone temple, shot from the top of a formation in Wonderland North.

Peering deep into Wonderland North.

SPRING WILDFLOWERS

Joshua Tree National Park boasts one of the most magnificent wildflower displays in the American Southwest. An astounding 750 species of flowering flora have been identified in the Park, representing two distinctly different desert ecosystems, the Sonoran Desert and the Mojave Desert.

Dormant seeds lie in wait for springtime showers when the desert comes alive with every color of the rainbow: deep magenta Hedgehog blooms, vibrant red Claret Cups, hot orange Mariposa Lilies, bright yellow Coreopsis, brilliant blue Canterbury Bells, rich violet Larkspur, and every shade and nuance between. You'll see wildflowers in every size and shape, from ground-cover plants that sprout flowers so tiny that they are hard to see without a magnifying glass, all the way up to giant nolinas with flower stalks that tower 10 feet into the air. Joshua trees themselves grow football-size flower clusters that earned them the name "Cabbage Palm" by Spanish settlers

Opposite top: Bright yellow *Narrowleaf Goldenbush* with purple *Wild Hyacinth*.
Opposite bottom: *Tulip Pricklypear* bloom.
Above top: Bugs-eye view of *Coreopsis*.
Above middle: *California Evening Primrose*.
Right side: Macro shot of *Parish's Larkspur* stalk.

in the early 1800s. By contrast, the Smoke Tree grows a tiny and delicate violet flower that from far away gives the tree a faint bluish hue. The ever-present creosote bush sprouts a yellow flower that is so small it might go unnoticed if it weren't for the unsettling buzz of hundreds of bees that crowd its spindly branches. Some flowers seem to be made out of rubber, like the "Live Forever" succulent, with its long pink stems and ornamental yellow bulbs. Others are furry, like the Bull Thistle, vibrantly standing its ground among all of the other pricklies with its four-foot-tall flower stalks and spiky disposition. Many wildflowers are wonderfully fragrant, but Chia bulbs will sneakily stink you if you brush against them. Some wildflowers have petals as delicate as the finest rose; others will hurt you if you get too close! One elegant white beauty has the power to drive admirers to madness: Datura, with its dangerously unpredictable psychotropic properties called upon in ancient times by Native Americans for their "vision quests."

Typically, the wildflowers of Joshua Tree begin their blooming season in March and intensify through April and May. Wetter years make for more intense displays, and may even produce

Top: *Desert Mariposa Lily* with dark shadows.
Middle: *Grizzly Bear Prickly Pear* blooms.
Bottom left: *Yucca* flower.
Botom middle: *Pinnate Prince's Plume* adorned with lady bugs.
Bottom right: *Bigelow's Monkeyflower*.
Opposite page: *Lupine* lollypops in the mist.

a second minor bloom in the fall. A few good hotspots to view wildflowers include the plains of Quail Springs, lower Geology Tour Road and Pleasant Valley beyond, and along the base of Queen Mountain.

Opposite Page
Top: Purple *Distant Phacelia* with yellow *Brittlebush* in the background.
Middle left: *Hedgehog Cactus* patch in full bloom.
Middle right: The desert rose, *Beavertail Prickly Pear*.
Bottom left: Tiny yellow *Bigelow's Tickseed* bellyflowers.

This Page
Top left: Vibrant orange *Desert Mallow*.
Lower left: Ornate purple and blue *Sage* flowers.
Top right: Details of a *Bull Thistle* flower.
Upper middle right: Peach hued *Dollarjoint Prickly Pear* blooms.
Lower middle right: Green *Silver Cholla* flower.
Bottom right: *Desert Sand Verbena*.

CHAPTER 2
CENTRAL JOSHUA TREE

Nighttime hustle and bustle at Intersection Rock.

Geographically speaking, the "center" of Joshua Tree is a bit further to the southeast than this area, but in terms of visitor interest, this is the hub of the Park. Towering rock piles rise straight up out of the flat desert, each one an island to be explored. Looking for adventure? Try the cavernous corridor "hike" of the Great Chasm, or go on a wild goose chase to find the Iron Door Cave. If those sound too adventurous, the Hidden Valley Loop Trail offers a pleasant walk through jagged crags and boulders. Visitors can also find excellent picnic sites scattered around the large parking loop. Central Joshua Tree is also home to the holy grail of campgrounds in the Park, Hidden Valley Campground.

Central Joshua Tree is most easily accessed from the West Entrance. From there, travel 8.8 miles east on Park Boulevard to reach the intersection at Intersection Rock. If coming from the North Entrance, drive west on Park Boulevard for 16.6 miles to reach Intersection Rock. From the South Entrance, travel to the Cottonwood Visitors Center and then continue on Pinto Basin Road, traveling northwest for 30 miles to the Pinto Wye junction with Park Boulevard. Turn left (W) on Park Boulevard and drive another 12 miles to reach Intersection Rock.

Opposite: Lost Horse Valley giant.

dirt turnout

Lost Horse Road

Park Boulevard

parking

Hemingway
Parking

parking

parking

Park

Hidden Valley
Loop Trail
6

The Great
Chasm
7

CENTRAL
JOSHUA TREE

Lost Horse Valley Link-Up **8**

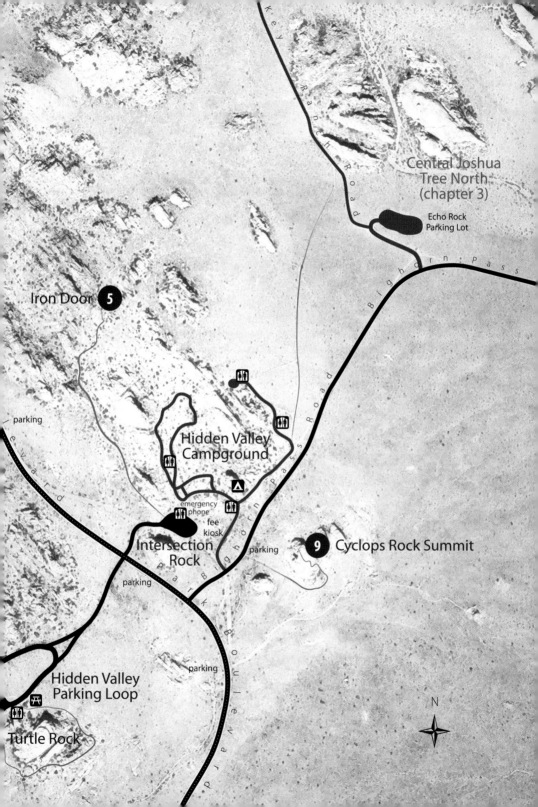

Central Joshua
Tree North
(chapter 3)

Echo Rock
Parking Lot

Iron Door 5

Hidden Valley
Campground

Cyclops Rock Summit 9

emergency
phone

fee
kiosk

Intersection
Rock

parking

parking

parking

parking

parking

Hidden Valley
Parking Loop

Turtle Rock

Keys Ranch Road

Bighorn Pass

Park Boulevard

Bighorn Pass Road

Park Boulevard

N

LOST HORSE ROAD

Round the bend at Keys Corner and the road straightens out a bit. The rock piles get denser as the road grazes the southern tip of the Wonderland of Rocks. At 7.5 miles (from West Entrance) is a dirt road on the right (S). This is Lost Horse Road. The road on the left (N) side leads into private property. Lost Horse Road leads south for about 0.5 miles before ending at a gate with a dirt parking area. (Past the gate, the road is closed to the public.) Lost Horse Road has many turnouts with small climber trails leading in and out of the rocky formations. One of the tallest rock formations in the Park, the Lost Horse Wall, is found near the end gate. There are restrooms at the junction of Park Boulevard and Lost Horse Road.

HEMINGWAY BUTTRESS

The Hemingway Buttress.

Just past Lost Horse Road, 7.7 miles from West Entrance, is this popular place to stop. A large parking lot with restrooms can be found here, as well as an information plaque noting rock climbing and the Hemingway Buttress. Hemingway Buttress is the large, pointy crag directly in front of the parking lot. If you're packing binoculars, dig them out! This craggy granite wall is one of the most popular locales for rock climbing in the Park. The main formation boasts around 50 different climbing routes, with another hundred or so on the cliffs and boulders in the surrounding area.

Looking east at Intersection Rock and its surrounding roads and parking areas.

A rock climber rappels from the top of Intersection Rock at sunset.

INTERSECTION ROCK

If central Joshua Tree is the hub of Joshua Tree National Park, then Intersection Rock is ground zero! The rock itself is a giant monolith of granite sitting out on the desert floor. Rock climbers can usually be seen strewn all across its flanks. Several of the climbing routes on this monolith date back to the 1940s , making them among the oldest technical rock climbs in the country. A large parking lot with restrooms and an emergency telephone can be found behind the rock, offering a good place to stop and soak up the ambiance of Joshua Tree National Park. The "intersection" is 8.8 miles from the West Entrance. Be prepared to slow to a halt as gawkers, fumbling for their cameras and iPhones, stop in the middle of the road to take photos of rock climbers on the towering Intersection Rock. A much better place to take photos is from a turnout just past the intersection, or just park in Intersection Rock parking lot and take a stroll around the rock! Turn left (N) at the intersection for Intersection parking lot.

Photography notes:
There many good photographic opportunities just outside of (and even inside) the Intersection Rock parking lot. Plan on being here in the late afternoon through sunset. Long shadows abound as the colors become richer, culminating in a full orange glow just before sundown. Many interesting Joshua trees can be found around the parking lot, making for nice silhouettes and other compositions. Another point of interest is the northwest tip of Intersection Rock: A rappel route there situates rock climbers perfectly on the horizon as they descend. Throw in a nice sunset with clouds, and voila! A postcard classic! Photographers will want to be on the far east end of the lot for the best angle.

HIKE
The Iron Door - #5

Total distance: 0.8 miles (round trip)
Physical difficulty: 1
Technical difficulty: 1
Navigating: 3
Trail type: cross-country/no trail

This is more of a wild goose chase than an actual hike. A bit of navigating will be required on a criss-crossing of small trails, and finding the door itself will require some hunting around (and luck). Due to its proximity to the campground, however, and the popularity of the area with rock climbers, there are usually people wandering around who are more than happy to point you back to the parking lot should you get lost.

The Iron Door is a strange relic from the mining era of Joshua Tree. It seals a natural cave in the rocks and is well hidden. Apparently nobody knows its true purpose, **although many yarns have been woven as to its nature. The most popular tale tells of a local homesteader locking his insane brother in the cave, far from his house so**

Granite castle and boulders. Inset: The infamous Iron Door Cave.

as not to hear his howling and ranting. Others surmise that it was built by miners for storing explosives under lock and key, although there are no mines anywhere nearby. Stories aside, it's just a door and there is not much to see here—the real adventure is in finding the thing!

Details: Head west from Intersection parking lot, walking along the base of the rock formation. Continue ahead (NW) to an obvious canyon entering the rock piles. Intermittent trails and deep sand lead into this canyon. Once in the rock piles, the sandy wash bends to the right (N), leading into a valley that opens up beyond. Continue along the wash past several points where rocks and bushes choke it. The wash, now small and intermittent, will dead end at some large boulders. (This cluster of boulders is very popular with rock climbers and often there are people climbing here. You will see their white gymnastic chalk spattered on the rock holds.) Scramble between the rocks and look for a wave-shaped overhang, with a piñon pine growing near it. If you are facing the overhanging wave, the Iron Door is in the rock directly behind you. Walk to the right side of that rock, looking down in the crevices—it is easy to walk straight past the door and not see it. Good Luck!

HIDDEN VALLEY

Another area that is very popular with visitors is Hidden Valley. The main attraction here is the Hidden Valley Loop Trail, which passes through the "hidden" entrance and into Hidden Valley proper, where you'll find a pleasant loop hike. The clanking and chattering of rock climbers can be heard all throughout this locale.

The parking loop offers park benches and barbecues, as well as restrooms. A spur loop at the south end of the larger loop has some excellent individual picnic sites that are nestled in among the rocks. Adventure seekers will want to check out the Great Chasm, a deep cleft that passes through one of the formations in front of the parking lot. Traversing it requires some easy spelunking

Nightscape, with clouds warmly lit by the city lights of nearby Palm Springs.

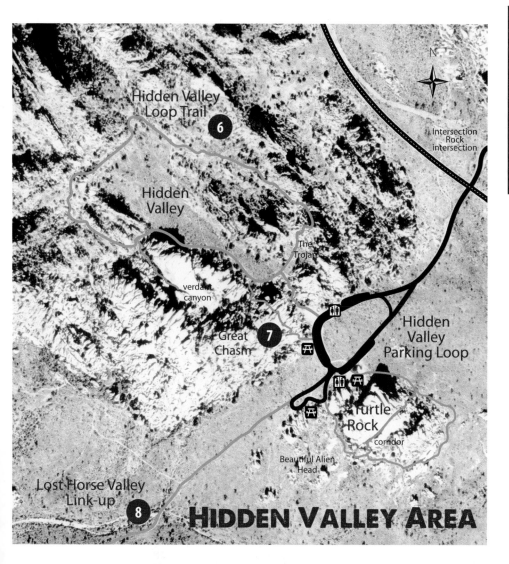

Hidden Valley
Loop Trail
6

Hidden
Valley

The
Trojan

verdant
canyon

Great
Chasm
7

Hidden
Valley
Parking Loop

Turtle
Rock

corridor

Beautiful Alien
Head

Lost Horse Valley
Link-up
8

N

Intersection
Rock
intersection

HIDDEN VALLEY AREA

and rock climbing—and an adventurous spirit! Several other deep corridors in the area offer more opportunities for exploration.

And finally, for visitors looking to get away from the crowds, the lonely Lost Horse Trail leads out into the open desert, passing a rock with faint pictographs, and then off toward rocky formations in the distance. Faint climber trails and an old dirt road can be found connecting this trail to small trails found near the end of Lost Horse Road.

Directions: The Hidden Valley parking area is located just off the "intersection" in central Joshua Tree. Turn south at the Intersection Rock intersection and follow the short paved road into the one-way parking loop. Hidden Valley and the Loop Trail are at the first restroom, the Great Chasm is at the bend in the lot, the spur loop is the right turn at the south end of the lot, and Turtle Rock is the large formation behind the second restroom on the east side of the parking loop. Note: In peak season this parking lot is sometimes filled to capacity.

HIKE

Hidden Valley Loop Trail - #6

Total distance: 1 mile
Physical difficulty: 1
Technical difficulty: 1
Navigating: 1
Trail type: official trail

This easy hike circles the inside of an enclosed valley lined with towering granite cliffs and rock piles. A "secret" path weaving through boulders leads into the valley. Cattle rustlers in the late 1800s used the hidden valley to stash stolen livestock. Several small catchments (dams) can be found around the valley. Today, rock climbers, bird watchers, and wandering visitors alike enjoy the valley's secluded charms. A short side-trek leads to a beautiful verdant slot canyon. Adverturous hikers can rock scramble to the summit of the gargantuan Sentinel Rock formation.

Details: Just left of the first restroom is a large information board noting the history

of Hidden Valley. The trail leads west from behind this board, almost immediately ducking into the rocks at the "hidden" entrance. Wind up through the rocks and the valley opens up, revealing a large flat area surrounded by towering rock piles. A small sign notes the official direction of the trail: counterclockwise. Turn right and follow the trail north, ascending into another rocky area. Note: Just before entering the rocky area, to its right, is the Trojan, a rock that resembles a helmeted Greek warrior.

Continuing on through the rocky area, the trail bends left (W) and begins to descend into a lower part of the valley. Wander the trail as it weaves around the rocky formations, eventually bending back toward the start of the loop, heading east. About three quarters of the way around the loop, the trail will pass between some small rock piles. A beautiful verdant canyon lies just off the trail to its right (E), tucked in behind one of the largest cliffs in the Park, the Sentinel. This canyon—one of the highlights of the entire trail—should not be missed! It is dense in foliage, with several large trees rising alongside the towering cliff. The back of the canyon pinches down to a deep corridor with seemingly impenetrable foliage. There, faint trails can be found leading easily to the back of the corridor. (It is possible to climb out at the end, but it's quite exposed and should only be attempted by experienced technical rock climbers.)

Back at the loop trail, continue following it as it travels below the west side of the Sentinel, to the sign at the start of the loop. Turn right (E) and scramble through the boulders to the parking lot. From the sign, it is also possible to walk up onto the "backbone" of the Sentinel: Turn south, walk 25 yards, then turn left into a brushy side canyon. A climber's trail will lead around a large round boulder and through the brush. Look for the backbone on the right. Use extreme caution if going to the summit of the Sentinel. The rounded cliff edges lead to a 200-foot drop to the desert floor! Small children should never be brought up here. Also, great care should be taken not to kick or throw anything off the sides. Rock climbers and visitors alike may be below. Rock fall can easily result in serious injury or death!

Opposite: Verdant slot-canyon found off of the Hidden Valley Loop Trail.
Below: Panoramic view of Hidden Valley from the summit of the Sentinel.

HIKE
The Great Chasm - #7

Total distance: 0.25 miles
Physical difficulty: 3
Technical difficulty: 4
Navigating: 3
Trail type: rock scrambling/no trail

Not for the faint of heart! The Great Chasm, also known as the Chasm of Doom, is a deep fissure that cleaves Gateway Rock, the formation just left of the start of the Hidden Valley Loop Trail. The crux of the Chasm is belly-crawling through a scant crevice and then tunneling upward toward light! Local traditional holds that the journey through the Chasm should be undertaken at night— but I won't hold you to that! This adventure involves about 0.25 miles of travel with moderately strenuous scrambling. On hot days the chasm can be 20 degrees cooler than the surrounding desert.

Details: If you are standing at the first restroom looking south, Gateway Rock is directly in front of you. The Great Chasm starts on the left horizon line of the formation. From the parking lot, head to the left edge of the Gateway Rock formation; there are a few concrete benches and barbecues located here. Scramble up into the rocks behind a concrete bench. Several very large boulders mark this location. Continue up behind the largest boulder, looking for the start of a groove with boulders lodged in the top. (A bit of hunting may be required here.) Scramble up the groove, under the boulders, until an impassable alcove is encountered. The large boulder blocking the way has a crevice at its base, about ankle high. Get down on your belly (or back) and start swimming into the darkness! After about 15 feet, you'll see a vertical shaft with a bit of light at the top. Go into the light! Climb out of the crevice and into another alcove. A deep chasm is located at the other

The main corridor of the Great Chasm.

end. Descend into the depths of the chasm, employing a few "chimney" moves to get to the lower base. At the opposite end of the chasm, large boulders choke the way. Tunnel under, over, and to the side of boulders until back on level ground. Exit the brush-filled side canyon, staying to the right (N). This will deposit you in Hidden Valley near the start of the loop. Turn right and then right again to return to the parking lot.

Looking across Lost Horse Valley to Ryan Mountain.

HIKE

Lost Horse Valley
Link-Up Trail - #8

Total distance: 1 mile
Physical difficulty: 1
Technical difficulty: 1
Navigating: 1
Trail type: large trail (unofficial)

Last light in Lost Horse Valley.

This rather large and inviting trail can be found leaving the southern tip of the parking lot spur loop. This is not an official trail, nor does it really lead anywhere, but just kind of fizzles out into the desert after about a half a mile. It does, however, pass a few interesting sights on its way into some beautiful Joshua tree country. A rock with some faint pictographs can be viewed just off the trail, and further along the trail fades into a Joshua tree forest where there are several giant trees. Wanderers then have the option of returning on the trail or striking off cross-country to explore several island rock piles that are located near the end of the trail.

Details: This trail is located at the southern tip of the parking lot spur loop. Walk to the end of the spur loop, then follow a well-trodden trail southwest into the open desert. There are also several smaller trails to the right and left of this one, closer to the rock formations. After a third of a mile the trail will cross through a wash, then pass

Picturesque Joshua trees at the southern side of Turtle Rock.

near a lonely rock pile on the left. Look for faint pictographs on the rock facing the trail here. Continue on ahead to a second sandy wash, about half a mile from the parking. Here you will find some of the largest and oldest Joshua trees in the Park. Veer right and head for the huge rock piles in the desert. Retrace your steps, or use one of many other small trails that lead back to the parking lot.

Compositional chaos shot in Lost Horse Valley.

Photography notes:
This part of Lost Horse Valley, as described in the hike, has some of the largest Joshua trees in the Park. The distant western horizon ensures long shadows in the afternoon, and at the opposite end of the valley are Ryan Mountain and the gargantuan Saddle Rock, making for an excellent background. The wide-open valley to the east also makes this a great location to be at sunrise.
Side trek: From the second sandy wash in the hike description, head right (W) to the first rock pile out in the open desert. It may take a bit of hunting around but there is an interesting natural window in a boulder lying on the desert floor. Several other egg-shaped boulders nearby make for lots of compositional possibilities.

TURTLE ROCK

Turtle Rock is the large formation east of the Hidden Valley parking loop. A small trail circles the rock, making for a pleasant walk. The south side of the rock has many large and oddly shaped boulders, rock spires, and Joshua trees to wander through and explore. This area is particularly beautiful in the late afternoon. Also, hidden in the large boulders close to the main formation, is the entrance to a secret corridor. The corridor cuts through the whole formation. Finding the entrance to the corridor is a bit tricky, but walking through is easy. A small trail weaves through brush to the corridor's end, where a scramble through a jumble of boulders leads back out.

Right: The Beautiful Alien Head rock formation.

HIDDEN VALLEY CAMPGROUND

Hidden Valley Campground is the holy grail of camping in Joshua Tree. Situated just across from Intersection Rock in the center of the universe, this campground offers hiking, exploring, rock scrambling, and rock climbing all within its grounds, not to mention a multitude of other areas just a stone's throw away. Set up camp here and you may never have to get back in your car for your entire stay! Unfortunately, scoring a site is next to impossible. The sites here are first-come, first-served and cannot be reserved. Your best bet is to prowl the campground on a Sunday night or Monday morning and hope you get lucky.

For those fortunate enough to bag a site at this campground, there are many areas of interest within walking distance as well as a few in the campground itself. Just to the west is a complex of rock piles known as the Outback. Across Bighorn Pass Road to the east is Cyclops Rock. To the south is Intersection Rock and beyond that, Hidden Valley. To the north is a link-up trail that leads first to Echo Rock, then on to Barker Dam and the Wonderland. Separating the inner loop from the back end of the outer loop is a long formation known as "the Wall." This formation has several possible paths leading to the summit. Another oddity in this area is a capsule-like hole in a rock high above and the campsites known as the Space Station.

From the West Entrance, travel southeast on Park Boulevard for approximately 8.8 miles to the intersection at Intersection Rock. Drive past this intersection to a road on the left (NE) about 200 yards further. This is the Barker Dam/Bighorn Pass Road. Turn left, then after about 50 yards turn left again into the campground. The fee box is just past the bend. Continue ahead to the next junction, where the road becomes dirt. Turning left will lead to the inner loop, while turning right heads around the outer loop. The sites in the inner loop are nestled among the rocks, whereas the outer loop sites look out onto open desert.

Campers eagerly await the warming sun on a crisp winter morning along the Inner Loop of Hidden Valley Campground..

THE SPACE STATION

The Space Station is a large cave-like feature about 30 feet up on a rock formation in the middle of the campground. The "hole" can fit several people comfortably, and it's not uncommon to see people sitting in it. However, the route leading up and into the Space Station is extremely dangerous and not recommended.

CYCLOPS ROCK

Just east of the campground is a cluster of large rock formations. The largest square-shaped formation in the middle is Cyclops Rock. Ever-present climber trails loop each of the formations here, and there is also a trail continuing east to the rock formations on the far hillside. It's possible to ascend Cyclops Rock without too much difficulty. See the Cyclops Rock Summit trail for more details on this area.

Cyclops Rock and Ryan Mountain dusted with snow and basking in sunset light.

HIKE

Cyclops Rock Summit - #9

Total distance: 0.4 miles
Physical difficulty: 3
Technical difficulty: 3
Navigating: 2
Trail type: climber trail/rock scrambling

Cyclops Rock is a prominent formation jutting 120 feet up from the desert floor and nestled among a group of smaller rocks at the edge of the open plain. The rock is named because of a natural window (the Eye), located at the top of a central cleft in the rock. This cleft happens to be one of the most popular easy rock climbs in the Park. The back of Cyclops Rock is like a big ramp, making it a fairly easy scramble to the summit. The summit offers a grand view of Hidden Valley Campground, Intersection Rock, and the surrounding area. Many come up here for sunset. The Eye is a cave-like area just below the summit. Take care not to drop debris down on rock climbers.

Details: Two hundred yards east of the "intersection" at Intersection Rock is a road that leads north: Bighorn Pass Road. Take Bighorn Pass Road north for a hundred yards or so and park at a long turnout on the right, just across from the entrance to Hidden Valley Campground. Cyclops Rock is the large square formation east of the turnout. Follow the main trail around the right side of the formation to its east side. (Past visitor impact here has devastated the area, so please stay on the main trail.) Start up somewhere on the middle right of the east side, scrambling over boulders to reach a ramp leading to the top. There is one difficult tier to overcome midway. Take care at the summit; it is a 120-foot drop to the desert floor. Also take care not to drop rocks or debris off the side as there are usually people walking around at the bottom of the formation.

ROCK CLIMBING 101

Rock climbing is indelibly linked to Joshua Tree National Park. Recorded climbing activity dates back to the 1940s. In a time when homesteaders and miners were still eking out a living on the craggy plains of the Park, rock climbers from the famed RCS (Rock Climbing Section) of the Sierra Club were surveying the many granite domes and outcrops, seeking a good winter destination to ply their trade. Pioneers of modern American rock climbing—Royal Robbins, Yvon Chouinard, and others—refined their skills and equipment on the diminutive rocks of Joshua Tree before going on to conquer the great cliffs of Yosemite. Little did they know that their "practice" area would eventually grow to be one of the most popular climbing destinations on the globe, eclipsing even the mighty Yosemite Valley in climbing popularity!

A rock climber nearing the top of a route known as "E.B.G.B.'s," on Echo Rock.

Placing cams is a strenuous business!

For those select climbers, though, Joshua Tree Monument was just a dusty oddity out in the middle of nowhere, and nobody then even bothered to record the climbing routes that were done. In the '60s, the hippy counter-culture forged an affinity with the strange realm of Joshua Tree, and the "Desert Rats Uninhibited" began recording their climbing routes, ultimately culminating in the first published guidebook for rock climbing in Joshua Tree (then only a National Monument). In the 1970s, the next wave of Joshua Tree climbers—the legendary Stonemasters—would push the very boundaries of the human mind, body, and spirit. Members of the Stonemasters include some of the greatest rock climbers of all time. John Bachar and Lynn Hill both spent many of their early years climbing in the Park. John would go on to climb many of the hardest free climbs on the planet— ropeless!—using skills honed on these modest rocks. Lynn would go on to win many climbing world championships and to do the first free ascent of what many consider the greatest rock climb on Earth, the Nose of El Capitan, in Yosemite. Today, Joshua Tree National Park is one of the top destinations the world over for rock climbing, popular primarily because of a wealth of easily accessible mild to moderately difficult routes. It is estimated that the Park has around 8000 recorded rock climbs.

So what exactly is going on up there? All that clanking and grunting and scraping against the wall? In the days of yore, the typical modus operandi was to Aid Climb. Aid Climbing basically involves taking pitons and other soft metal wedges, hammering them into cracks and seams, then clipping into an etrier (a nylon sling with a row of loops), standing as high as possible in it, then hammering in another piton as high as possible, clipping another etrier into that one, and standing once again as high as possible, repeating the process to the top. Rope and harnesses were integral to the process, not just used for safety. For the modern climber, the object is to use only one's body (hands, feet, muscle) and the natural holds and features of the rock to ascend the cliff. Rope, gear, and harnesses are used for protection only, to safeguard the climber in case of a slip. The goal of most climbers these days is to ascend the

entire rock climb without falling or resting any body weight on the rope or gear. A climber will continue to attempt a route over and over until this is accomplished. The purpose of the rope and hardware is simply to allow the climber to survive the falls and try again!

Modern gear includes camming devices that contract with the squeeze of a trigger, allowing the climber to slide the device into cracks or slots. When the trigger is released, the "cam" sits firmly in place. A strong downward pull, such as a falling person, will cause the device to expand with great force against the sides of the crack, holding thousands of pounds with ease. To remove the device, a squeeze of the trigger suffices. Climbers also use soft metal wedges, called nuts, that are fiddled into constrictions where they just kinda sit. It sounds sketchy, but they are actually quite solid. And finally there are bolts, permanent points of protection that are installed where no other gear can be utilized. Back in the day, climbers would install bolts as a last measure as they scaled a rock face, sometimes clinging

Very old (and unsafe) protection bolts.

precariously at a meager stance for 20 minutes or more as they hand-drilled small holes before hammering in the bolt. These days, climbers typically rappel down, installing them while hanging on the rope before actually climbing the route. The installation of bolts is now carefully regulated within the Park.

For a select few brave souls, there is "free soloing"—NOT to be confused with free climbing (although it often is by non-climbers). Free soloing, or "soloing," employs no safety ropes or gear. The movement is the same as in free climbing, but there is no protection in the case of a fall. For some climbers, free soloing is the ultimate expression of rock climbing, free from the rope and all the distracting gear, employing only flesh and stone, coupled with experience, ability, and conditioning to overcome the dizzying heights. Some may view this to be more foolish than brave! Climbers typically only solo routes that they have climbed many times before, are quite familiar with the terrain, and are totally confident in their ability to reach the top (and also in their ability to climb back down to the ground, should they need to). The small size of many of Joshua Tree's rocks, and the ease of walking off the backsides, makes soloing in the Park fairly common.

Falling is common in modern climbing!

"Bouldering" is the latest craze in rock climbing. No confusing jargon here—it's just what it sounds like: climbing on boulders. Originally thought of as "practice" for real climbing, bouldering exploits rocks too small for ropes, ranging in size from 10 to 25 feet tall. Freed from the burden of fidgeting with protection gear, and close enough to the ground to jump or fall, the boulderer can focus purely on physical difficulty. The most difficult climbing "moves" in the world are all on boulders. Unlike soloing, bouldering involves falling often, as the climber tries over and over again to unlock a difficult sequence of moves. To prevent broken ankles and such, boulderers use large "crash pads" that they lay on the ground below the climb. A crash pad is

Cams come in a variety of types; colors help climbers quickly pick the right size.

A boulderer pushes herself to the physical limit, relying on 'crashpads' to cushion the ground in case of a fall.

basically a large piece of foam with a colorful cover over it; they come fitted with shoulder straps for carrying. Most visitors to the Park will at some point see a group of people filing along, like a walking deck of cards, with the large, blocky crash pads strapped to their backs. Yup, that's what those "mattresses" are for!

Gymnastic moves close to the ground are the name of the game in bouldering.

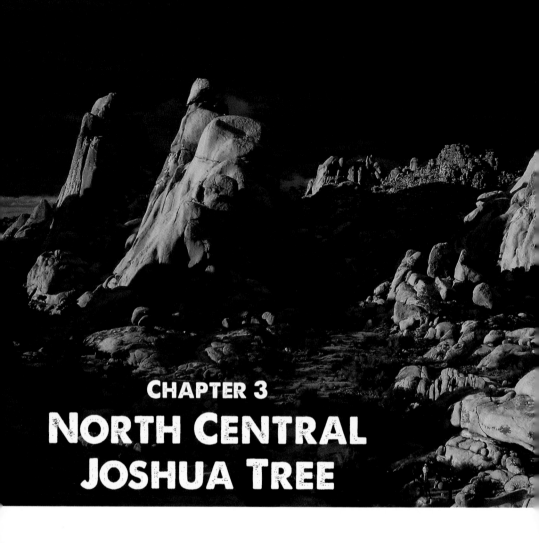

CHAPTER 3
NORTH CENTRAL JOSHUA TREE

The northern portion of central Joshua Tree is distinct enough to warrant its own chapter. From the large dome of Echo Rock, oftentimes festooned with rock climbers, to the fascinating Keys Ranch and its windows into the past, to the southern Wonderland of Rocks, replete with Native American pictographs and homesteader ruins, there is something here for everybody. This region is accessed by turning onto Bighorn Pass Road, 200 yards east of the "intersection" at Intersection Rock on Park Boulevard. The turn is 8.9 miles from the West Entrance and 17 miles from the North Entrance. Bighorn Pass Road travels north before bending to the northeast and dead-ending at the Barker Dam Parking Lot approximately 2 miles further. Before Barker Dam, at mile 1, is a dirt road on the left that leads west to Keys Ranch. Just before the Barker Dam parking lot is another dirt road, on the right; this road leads to the South Wonderland parking and also into Queen Valley (see Chapter 5).

Late afternoon sunshine sneaks in under a winter storm in the Wonderland of Rocks.

ECHO ROCK

The Echo Rock area, also known as Echo T, is an area of tall rock formations with open desert and deep sandy washes in between. The trails here generally tread flat ground and washes unless you decide to scramble into one of the many irresistible rock piles. The area is is laced with climber trails, and in general a trail can be found encircling each rock formation. Only the most prominent trails will be outlined here. To reach the Echo Rock area, travel Bighorn Pass Road for 1 mile to a dirt road on the left (W); this is Keys Ranch Road, and you are at the Echo T. Turn here and then almost immediately turn right into a large dirt parking lot. Restrooms can be found here. There are also more parking turnouts farther along Keys Ranch Road.

HIKE

Echo Rock Loop Trail - #10

Total distance: 1 mile
Physical difficulty: 1
Technical difficulty: 1
Navigating: 2
Trail type: mixed climber trails

This easy 1-mile walk circles the largest single chunk of rock in the area, Echo Rock. The backside of the formation is lush with piñon and turbinella oak, mixed in with boulders, caves, and alcoves. Signs of Native American life can be found here and there. High-place adventurers can take a side excursion that branches off from this trail and leads up to the summit of Echo Rock. The return trail passes below one of the most popular cliffs in the Park for rock climbing, giving wanderers a close-up view of the action.

Details: This trail begins by following the Barker Dam Link-up Trail for 300 yards. The trail will cross a large wash, then pass to the right of the massive Echo Rock. Look for a small climber trail veering off to the left behind Echo Rock, contouring the base of the formation. Follow this trail northwest as it continues around the rock. At a deep, sandy wash, turn left (SW) and follow the wash back toward the parking lot. An obvious trail will complete the last stretch to the lot.

NORTH CENTRAL JOSHUA TREE

Keys Ranch

Keys parking

Barker

Echo Rock Loop

10

parking

parking

12

Ec Su

Echo Rock Parking Lot

to Hidden Valley

Echo Tee

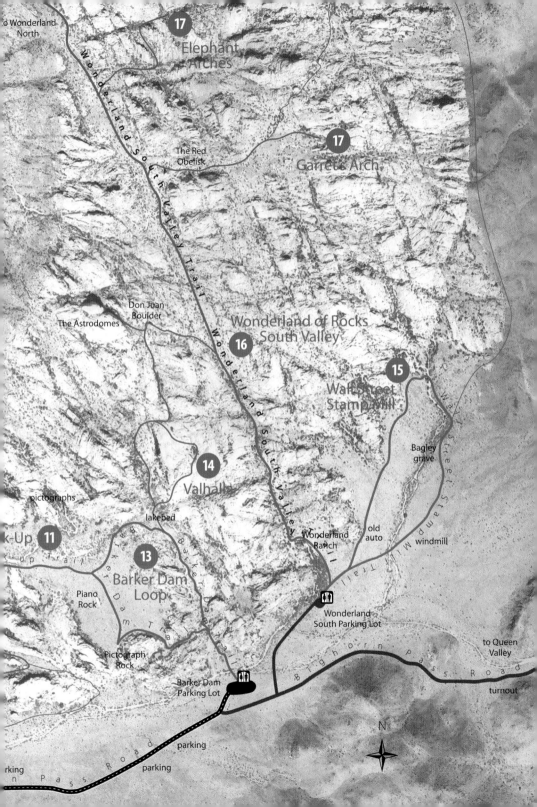

Massive granite formations, called Inselbergs, jut out of the ground at Echo Tee. Echo Rock is the large formation on the right.

HIKE

Barker Dam Link-Up - #11

Total distance: 1 mile
Physical difficulty: 1
Technical difficulty: 1
Navigating: 2
Trail type: official trail

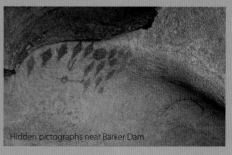

Hidden pictographs near Barker Dam.

This hike has shorter and longer variations. It starts at the Echo T parking lot and passes between several large rock formations before heading into an enclosed valley where it meets the Barker Dam Loop Trail at about its midpoint. The area is peppered with verdant nooks and cul-de-sacs, and signs of Native American life can be found throughout the valley.

Details: Locate the trailhead at the northeast corner of the parking lot. Take the trail northeast. After 100 yards you will merge with another, more prominent, spur trail that begins near Echo T proper. Bear left (N) and follow the larger trail, leading through a sandy wash and then past the massive Echo Rock formation, continuing on into the desert behind. After another 400 yards, the trail will drop into a sandy wash, passing near a low dome of granite called the Little Hunk. The link-up trail then heads out into the middle of an enclosed valley to meet up with the Barker Dam Loop Trail (0.75 miles from the parking lot).

If you want to head straight to Barker Dam from here, go left for another quarter mile. If you plan on walking the whole Barker Dam Loop, it may be better to go right at the junction and walk the loop that way, as it is easier to navigate. Total distance for the link-up and the Barker Dam Loop Trail is 2.5 miles round trip.

An interesting alternative is to veer right (E) about 200 yards before the low dome of granite, heading for a tight canyon between the long Little Hunk formation and a small formation. This small canyon has some beautiful manzanita trees, as well as piñon pine and turbinella oak. At the opening to the canyon, one can find remnants of a homestead, or possibly a small cattle operation. Glass, tin cans, barbwire, wood, and other objects litter the ground. Note: This "junk" is considered artifactual, and protected by law, so please do not remove anything! Continue through the canyon to where it opens up. At this point, one can hook around to the right, pass over a notch, and head back to the parking lot. It's a 1-mile round trip for this route. Alternately, continue straight (E) into a much larger canyon with tall cliffs and overhangs on both sides. At the end of this canyon, a sandy wash will lead east into a small canyon and then down through a rocky notch to the open desert on the other side. Once on flat ground, turn to the right (S) and walk along the edge of the rock formations. (Bighorn Pass Road will be to your left, paralleling the trail.) After several hundred yards Echo Rock and the parking lot will come into view. Take any one of several small trails that will lead you back to the parking lot. Total distance for this route is 1.2 miles.

Adventurous highliners walk a gap at Echo Rock.

HIKE

Echo Rock Summit - #12

Total distance: 1 mile
Physical difficulty: 3
Technical difficulty: 4
Navigating: 2
Trail type: steep rock scrambling/no trail

Warning: This trek involves some perilous scrambling up steep terrain. Only experienced cross-country travelers should attempt it. The path also crosses above an area that is almost always crowded with people; avoid kicking off any debris, since even small rocks become bullets by the time they reach the ground. please be very careful and aware!

The 360-degree view from the summit is grand, with vistas including central Joshua Tree, Ryan Mountain, the Western Territories of the Park, and the southern edge of the Wonderland of Rocks, as well as a peek into the inner Wonderland itself. The summit of Echo Rock boasts a small desert-bonsai garden.

Details: Take the trail from the parking lot that leads north toward the left end of the Echo Rock dome. After a few hundred yards the trail drops into a sandy wash that leads along the base of the dome. Continue down the wash until a small trail leads out of the wash and to the right, up into an alcove with piñon pines. At the back of this alcove is a pile of large boulders spilling down the dome. Scramble/tunnel up these boulders (beware: some of the crevices here are deep!) until it's possible to traverse onto the dome. Continue to scramble up and to the right, heading to the dome's right shoulder. Several "ruts" will have to be crossed to continue. Eventually, a large flat area will be gained. (Be very careful not to kick debris off the side of the cliff here as this is directly above the rock-climbing cliff.) Atop this flat area is a large boulder with a cleft behind it. Cross this cleft, which requires climbing down a six-foot step, then surmounting a six-foot bulge on the other side. Remember that you have to reverse this to get back, so if this section seems like too much, turn back now. Once on the other side of the cleft, continue up the ramp, which eventually turns into a long backbone that leads to the summit.

The sprawling Keys Ranch: The main house is pictured below, with the garden in the middle and the machine shop at the far right.

KEYS RANCH

Keys Ranch offers a fascinating insight into the hardscrabble life of a homestead family living on the desert frontier of the American Southwest. The site is packed with innovations and adaptations for overcoming the adversities of life in this harsh place. The ranch is also a museum of all things abandoned in the desert, as Bill Keys would bring home anything he found in the area, including old mining equipment, bits of glass, and wrecked autos.

The Ranch is accessed by guided tour only, which at press time cost $5. Tour times and frequency are subject to change depending on interest, so check at one of the Park entrance kiosks for tour availability. If you pay the tour fee at one of the Park entrance kiosks, credit/debit cards are accepted; cash is required to pay at the Keys Ranch gate. Tours usually last about an hour.

Typically, tour guides will lead a procession of visitors in their own vehicles to a parking area at the ranch. From there, visitors are led on foot past an area of Native American cultural significance before walking onto the ranch proper. The ranch has several structures, including the original McHaney adobe house, the Keys' main house, the machine shop, several barns and sheds, and a small schoolhouse. Unfortunately, at the time of writing, only one barn is open for public viewing. The interiors of the main house, a larger barn, and the schoolhouse will all remain a mystery. Outside, though, the tour roams all over the grounds, viewing gardens, a well, a windmill, catchment dams, and other ingenious necessities. The tour usually ends at Bill Keys' storage yard, where all sorts of vintage machinery, autos, and frontier bric-a-brac can be found.

Well pulley and bucket at Keys Ranch.

Old mining wagons at Keys Ranch.

BILL KEYS AND JOSHUA TREE NATIONAL PARK

If there was ever a true Joshua Tree local, then Bill Keys was that person! He spent the better part of his life homesteading, working, prospecting, milling, scavenging, and helping to shape the local community in the high plateau of what is now Joshua Tree National Park. Keys built dams, established roads, and hosted a schoolhouse on his property. He staked claims, took over mines, pillaged abandoned operations, and also ran some of the higher-profile mines in the area. Bill also established and later owned the Wall Street Stamp Mill, running it for many years.

Bill Keys entered the area as a young man in around 1910. With a background in mining, he took on the job of superintendent at the Desert Queen Mine. In his off hours, Keys would spend time at a quiet alcove located in a valley west of the mine. The alcove, which had previously been the site of a McHaney mill, still contained an abandoned adobe structure and a well. Bill pitched his tent next to the well and ended up spending the rest of his life at the site. The Desert Queen Ranch, as he would later christen it, became the center of Bill Keys' universe.

In 1915, with substantial back pay owed, Keys took ownership of the Desert Queen Mine, cementing his residency in this dusty corner of the Mojave. Back at the ranch, Bill's quest to build a comfortable homestead intensified. He improved his well, constructed a dam, and built a house. He later brought in milling equipment and ran a mill at the site. Keys also embarked on a life-long obsession of collecting machinery and other objects discarded in the desert.

Eventually, Bill Keys met a girl, got married, and somehow convinced her to live out at the Desert Queen Ranch. Francis May Keys, a city girl by all accounts, readily took to the harsh, primitive way of life. Mrs. Keys grew a fine garden of both fruits and vegetables, canning enough to last the entire year. She tended cows, goats, and chickens, running the ranch while Bill was off mining, building roads, constructing dams, and performing other local services. Somehow the couple found time to have seven children, three of which died at a young age. Raising four children in this harsh, remote place, some 50 miles from the nearest civilization, was quite an accomplishment.

Mr. and Mrs. Keys continued to improve their way of life, inventing all sorts of ingenious adaptations to take full advantage of the meager resources available to them. Bill built a machine shop on the property, offering his services to the local community. He also constructed a schoolhouse at the ranch and hired an instructor. The school eventually served the entire area, for which the county reimbursed him. Bill Keys continued to build roads, construct dams, and took over an estimated 35 abandoned mines and claims in the surrounding valleys and hills.

In 1930, Keys bought a property at the far north end of Lost Horse Valley consisting of a well, a cabin, and the remains of a small ore-crushing operation. Along with two other partners, Keys constructed a mill operation, using equipment salvaged from other mines in the area—a two-stamp from Piñon Well, the engine works from Pushawalla, and a 12-horsepower gasoline engine from the Paymaster Mine—naming the operation the Wall Street Stamp Mill. The mill serviced many of the local mines, crushing ore for the Black Eagle, Elton Mine, Gold Crown, Golden Bee, and other smaller claims. In 1942, due to World War II, a mandate was issued to cease all non-essential mining activity, forcing the Wall Street Stamp Mill to close its doors.

Bill Keys also had a reputation for being a "bad hombre" with a short fuse and not one to be messed with. Keys would eventually pay the price for his short temper. In an ongoing quarrel with neighboring homesteader Worth Bagley over a stretch of road, the two ended up in a shootout on the high plains of Joshua Tree. Keys shot Bagley dead and was tried and convicted of murder, spending five years of his senior life behind bars before being exonerated. (See side story, Shootout in the Desert, page 107.)

Bill Keys and his cat at Keys Ranch.

During Bill Keys' time in prison, Francis Keys held down the fort. Her kids now grown and living elsewhere, she lived out at the Desert Queen Ranch alone, waiting for her husband to someday come home. At age 69, Bill finally did come home, and immediately went back to his active life, scavenging abandoned mines, repairing the dilapidated Desert Queen Ranch, and extending the top of Barker Dam. In their final years, the Keys played host to a growing number of recreational users of the newly created Joshua Tree National Monument surrounding the ranch. In 1963, Francis May Keys died. Bill would go on living for another six lonely years, dying in June of 1969, his body laid to rest in a small cemetery near the mouth of the alcove where he had spent most of his life, next to his wife and three of their children.

Piñon pine snag near Barker Dam.

WONDERLAND OF ROCKS SOUTH END, BARKER DAM AREA

The southern end of the Wonderland of Rocks labyrinth is friendlier to visitors than its other boundaries, with parking lots that go right up against the edge of the granite belt, and several well-marked and easy-to-explore trails. The Barker Dam Trail is among the most popular trails in the Park, weaving through rock corridors, past an unusual seasonal lake, and into an enclosed valley with Native American sites containing pictographs and grinding holes. The Wonderland South Trail passes an old homesteader ruin, then ducks into a long wash that leads trekkers into the very heart of the Wonderland. There is also a wonderfully preserved stamp mill, several abandoned vehicles, and even a gravesite

Water, earth, sky. Sunset reflecting on the water at Barker Dam Lake.

marking an infamous shootout.

The area has two parking lots to launch from: The large (paved) Barker Dam parking lot, and just beyond that, the less-developed Wonderland South parking lot. A short 0.3 miles trail links the two lots, so it's possible to access all the trails from either lot. Both parking lots have restroom facilities.

From the Echo T junction, take Bighorn Pass Road northeast for 2 miles as the pavement bends to the right (E) and then ends at the large Barker Dam parking lot. Just before this lot is a dirt spur road on the right, this is actually the continuation of Bighorn Pass Road. To reach the Wonderland South parking lot, turn right onto this dirt road, go 100 yards, then turn left onto another dirt road. Follow this to the lot. Staying on the dirt portion of Bighorn Pass Road will take you through the namesake pass and then into Queen Valley.

HIKE

Barker Dam Loop Trail - #13

Total distance: 1.5 miles
Physical difficulty: 1
Technical difficulty: 1
Navigating: 1
Trail type: official trail

This popular trail enters the southern edge of the Wonderland of Rocks, passing through a narrow gap between two granite formations to gain an enclosed valley that forms a natural catchment for water. At the south end of this valley is the historic Barker Dam. In wetter years, this catchment becomes filled to capacity with a beautiful (if murky) lake. Large,

Fall colors and granite reflections at Barker Dam Lake.

low-angle domes surround the lake, making for a surreal desert scene. The downstream side of the dam is usually lush with cattails and tall grasses. Several water troughs can also be found, remnants from the cattle-ranching days in the Park. Once past the dam, the trail enters another enclosed valley as it curves back toward the parking lot. The valley is dotted with areas of cultural significance, as well as Piano Rock, an odd lone rock sitting in the middle of the open desert. The story goes that cattle ranchers would entertain from atop this rock, using it as a stage of sorts. They even went so far as to drag a piano up onto the rock, where it sat for some time.

The trail then passes by Pictograph Rock, which features many pictographs and petroglyphs around an elevated cave area. Unfortunately, the vibrant paint on the rock art is not authentic. The original rock art was painted over in the mid-19th century for a Hollywood film production, long before historic preservation was a concern. There are, however, a few pieces of rock art that remain undisturbed. Note that the small canyon behind the rock has some beautiful stands of old manzanita.

Top: The "dry" side of Barker Dam, aka Bighorn Dam.
Middle: Barker Dam inscription, etched by Bill Keys.
Bottom: Water-conserving cattle trough.

Details: This trail starts at the west end of the parking lot, just left of the restrooms. There is a large information board at the trailhead. Take the trail west as it enters a gap in the rock formations. Continue straight as the trail weaves through scrub oak and boulders in the tight gap that eventually opens up into the enclosed valley that holds Barker Dam Lake—0.4 miles from the trailhead to here. Skirt left along the lake to reach the dam; the trail is sometimes hard to see in this rocky area. The dam itself, and the area immediately surrounding the base, are currently closed because of a graffiti problem. Apparently it has become fashionable for everyone to etch their names in the soft mortar of the dam and on the decaying rocks nearby! Needless to say, this is vandalism, it's illegal, and please don't do it!

Photography notes:
Barker Dam Lake is an area with much potential for photography. Whether or not the lake is filled, the permanent presence of moisture creates an oasis that attracts wildlife, including Bighorn sheep. If you are lucky enough to be here when the lake is partially or completely full, than you may come away with some truly stunning images. As always, plan on being here around sunrise or sunset. The high reflectivity of the water combined with the granite domes and boulders makes for some brilliant possibilities. In the fall, many of the trees here turn bright yellow.

Authentic petroglyphs mixed with "forged" glyphs and paintings.

From the dam, the trail drops down into a second enclosed valley and travels along a large wash before reaching a junction. The right junction links up with the Echo Rock Loop Trail; keep left. Follow the trail as it crosses the valley, past Piano Rock, then straight to Pictograph Rock.

From Pictograph Rock, the main trail heads north, back toward the parking lot, skirting along the base of cliffs, where more rock art can be found. Enter a narrow corridor that leads back to a trail junction near the start of the loop. Turn right (E) to get back to the parking lot.

Side Trek:
Indian Wave Boulders: This group of large boulders is located just west of the Barker Dam parking lot (that's behind the restroom for those directionally challenged). A small trail to the right of the restroom leaves the parking lot and enters a wash, veering to the right. The boulders are on the left side of this wash. Walk the trail for about 200 yards in the wash, then head to the tallest boulder on the right side of the group. Be mindful not to walk through any restoration areas, which are

marked with signs. On the back of this tall boulder is a cave formed by another boulder. The cave has a really nice ochre pictograph of a female wearing a dress. One of several found in the Park, the image possibly signifies encounters with early settlers. The cave also has several metates, including a very interesting set of smaller ones clustered together. It has been speculated that these holes could be a calendar of sorts. An opening in the roof allows a sliver of light to enter the cave, and as the seasons change, the light hits different holes. The area has a few other pictographs scattered around on the boulders, but they are faint and difficult to find. The other side of the boulder group has a concrete slab and a 30-foot stripe of tar on one of the boulders. These lovely additions are courtesy of the same Hollywood film crew that painted over the pictographs on the Barker Dam Loop.

Top: Metates and divots form a possible calendar.
Right: The Red Lady, a pictograph located in the same hollow as the metate calendar.

Curious bighorn sheep near Barker Dam.

HIKE

Valhalla - #14

Total distance: 1.5 miles
Physical difficulty: 1
Technical difficulty: 4
Navigating: 2
Trail type: steep rock scrambling/
no trail

This hike gains the flat summit of one of the domes that surrounds the lake at Barker Dam, offering breathtaking views of the Wonderland of Rocks and the lake. The top of the dome is long and flat, about the size of two football fields, and has several beautiful desert bonsai gardens and other areas to explore. A casual walk around the summit rim can bring you close to the remote Wonderland without having to endure the endless boulder hopping that is usually a prerequisite. This hike has some very steep scrambling and should only be attempted by competent off-trail hikers.

Details: Take the Barker Dam Loop Trail directly to the dam. Once the trail opens up to reveal the lake, look to the right (E) and identify a large, low-angle granite dome. The lake, or signs of the water line, should go right up to its base. Just left (W) of this dome is a second low-angle granite dome; this is Valhalla. The approach from here is dependent on water level. If the lake is low or dry, simply walk through the lakebed (N) and head straight to the southern tip of the Valhalla Dome. There is a string of boulders spilling down from the top of the dome here. Head up the dome to the right of this string of boulders. This is the technical/difficult part. Ascend about 50 feet of steep but featured rock, followed by another 100 feet or so of less-steep but still-strenuous hiking to reach the flat summit. If the lake is half full, walk around the right side (N) to get to the base of the dome. This may

Top: Barker Dam Lake as seen from the Valhalla area.
Lower: Sculpted rock in the Valhalla area.

require a bit of bushwhacking and hunting for a path leading through trees and thickets. If the lake is completely full, head over to the dam and cross on the dry side (walking across the dam is prohibited), then continue back, under and over boulders until it's possible to walk to the southern tip of Valhalla Dome. This option is very tedious and difficult. Hike distance is 1.5 miles round trip.

A dwarf piñon pine grows out of a crack in a granite dome, while a storm front looms in the background.

WONDERLAND OF ROCKS SOUTH END, WONDERLAND OF ROCKS SOUTH PARKING LOT

This dirt parking lot is the launch point for deep forays into the Wonderland. It is also the best starting point for the Wall Street Stamp Mill hike. The many nooks and alcoves along the edge of the massive sea of granite, and the open desert to the northeast of the lot, hide all sorts of interesting items: rolls of barbed wire, abandoned trucks and roadsters, crumbling remains of homesteads, even gravestones.

From Echo T, take Bighorn Pass Road north for 2 miles as it bends to the right (E) and then dead-ends at the Barker Dam parking lot. Just before this lot is a dirt road on the right; this is actually the continuation of Bighorn Pass Road. Turn on this dirt road and then turn left after 100 yards to enter the Wonderland South parking lot. Staying on the dirt portion of Bighorn Pass Road will lead through the namesake pass and then into Queen Valley.

HIKE

The Wall Street Stamp Mill - #15

Total distance: 2 miles
Physical difficulty: 2
Technical difficulty: 1

Navigating: 1
Trail type: official trail

This easy loop trail may be the most interesting hike in Joshua Tree National Park. The walk meanders along the edge of the towering piles of granite boulders that mark the rim of the Wonderland of Rocks, passing odd relics and abandoned bric-a-brac from Joshua Tree's sordid past. The well-marked trail first passes a strange and pretty ruin tucked away in a verdant alcove. Referred to as the Wonderland Ranch by some and Uncle Willie's Health Food Store by others, the ruin's official designation is the Ohlson Property. Not much is left of the structure save for a couple of crumbling walls, a chimney, a few bed frames, and lots of debris scattered around. A few of the remaining walls are painted a striking pink, which offers a bold contrast to the muted palette of the desert. From the ruins, the trail heads out into the open desert. Some may notice a rusty old truck to the left. This truck marks the final leg of the return loop described here. The wide main trail, which is actually an old road, now leads to a scant ruin out on the desert plain, marked by a barely standing windmill. Not much to see here, just a pile of rubble. The trail then veers back toward the rocks, passing the gravestone of Worth Bagley (see side story, page 107) before dropping into a verdant wash that leads directly to the Wall Street Stamp Mill. (Note: In late 2014, vandals smashed the gravestone into several pieces, which were later removed by the Park Service.) The well-preserved mill is on

(continue)

The Wall Street Stamp Mill.

An old truck near the Wonderland Ranch

(continued)

the National Register of Historical Sites. The name came from a nearby claim called the Wall Street Mine. Bill Keys took over the claim after it was abandoned, bringing in the stamp mill and other equipment. The mill ran for over 30 years, processing ore from local miners. The entire mill is fenced off and entry is prohibited. The area is rife with abandoned objects, junk, equipment, and even several old roadsters.

The return path described below takes a faint unofficial trail that skirts the rocks,

The Wonderland Ranch under the stars.

A desert "picture window."

leading past one final point of interest, a rusty old truck sitting on the desert floor. Alternatively, return on the official trail.

Details: Take the large trail that starts in the north corner of the Wonderland South parking lot, left of the restroom. After about 100 yards there will be a spur trail on the left. This trail leads 200 yards to the Wonderland Ranch. Back on the main trail, continue ahead as the trail veers to the right (NE), heading out into the open desert. The windmill and small ruin are 0.3 miles distant. From there, the trail will start to veer back to the left toward the rocks and hillside. After another 0.25 miles or so, look for the marked site where the gravestone was,

P hotography notes:

The Wonderland Ranch: This ruin is a must-visit for any aspiring Joshua Tree photographer. The vivid pink and white of the ruin's crumbling walls "pop" against the muted backdrop of the desert. The still-standing chimney and connected wall have a surreal quality about them as they sit in the open air with a grand view of the Wonderland all around. Another wall has a doorway and window that are perfect for framing various elements of the desert background. A bit of poking around in the bushes and the surrounding alcove will reveal many other odds and ends worth photographing—and don't pass up the rusty old truck further along on the main trail to the left. It has a strong presence sitting on the edge of the open desert.

which will be just off the trail to the left. The trail then follows alongside a wash for another 300 yards to the mill, which will be left of the wash. Junk will start to appear in the wash near the mill. The official trail returns as you came, but a nicer alternative is to take a faint trail that skirts the rocks heading south. This trail passes several deep alcoves, the second of which contains an old house foundation. After the second alcove, look for a rusty old truck. Just past the truck, rejoin the main trail leading to the parking lot.

Signs of ancient inhabitants.

Worth Bagley's gravestone. The green paint is from past vandalism. The stone was later broken by vandals and removed.

Shootout in the Desert:

Midway between the well and the mill is the site of an infamous showdown between neighboring homesteaders Worth Bagley and Bill Keys, evidenced by a lonely gravestone alongside the road (now gone; destroyed by vandals). The story, touted by LA press as being the last great shootout of the Wild West, went something like this: Keys and Bagley disliked each other right from the start. Keys owned the Wall Street Stamp Mill and had worked the site for quite some time, even building the original road out to the place. At some point, Bagley came to own a stretch of the land through which the road crossed. Bagley had warned Keys on several occasions to stay off his land, going so far as to drag obstacles into the road, and even lacing it with nails. Keys continued to use the road until one day, upon returning from the mill, he found the road blocked. When Keys got out of his car to remove the obstacles, Bagley approached with revolver in hand. Keys ran back to the car for his rifle, shots were fired, and when the dust settled, Worth Bagley lay dead in his tracks!

A rock climber ascends the North Astrodome, high above the Wonderland of Rocks.

HIKE

Wonderland of Rocks South Valley - #16

Total distance: 2 miles
Physical difficulty: 2
Technical difficulty: 2

Navigating: 2
Trail type: climber trail

This is the easiest path into the inner Wonderland of Rocks. The wash it travels cuts straight as an arrow into the belly of the immense maze of granite, through sheer-walled canyons dotted with intermittent pools of water. The trail weaves around tall boulders with odd and eerie shapes, and through old stands of turbinella oak and piñon pine. Eventually the canyon opens up into a broad valley lined with towering granite domes. Two of the largest rock formations in the Park can be found here, the Astrodomes. The clanking chatter of rock climbers can often be heard on the domes' steep flanks, as several of Joshua Trees best rock climbs are found here. Bighorn sheep also frequent this part of the Park. Keep a sharp eye out along the tops of the cliffs, where their heads occasionally pop up as they curiously peer over to observe us noisy humans below. There is also a secret passage leading to Barker Dam for those

bold enough to try to find it, guarded by one of the largest freestanding boulders in Joshua Tree.

Details: From the Wonderland South Parking Lot, left of the restroom, take the large trail heading north. After about 100 yards, take the trail that branches off to the left (N), which leads to the Wonderland Ranch. Once at the Ranch, follow a small trail left of the pink ruin as it turns left and ducks into a grove of oak trees. There is a small kiln here. Once through the trees, the trail enters a deep, sandy wash and soon after joins with another wash in a large sandy area. Turn right and follow the sandy wash north. For the next several hundred yards the trail intermittently exits and reenters the wash, depending on the amount of water there is. Continue in this wash for about 0.6 miles (0.75 miles from parking), until the canyon opens up into the broad Wonderland South Valley. At this point it may be a good idea to scramble up to a high point and have a look around to get your bearings. The main wash continues on straight to the northwest. The giant Astrodomes are to the left, on the west side of the valley. At this point, there are two options: You can continue along in the main wash, which becomes smaller through this area (see Garret's Arch and Elephant Arches hikes, next page, for description from here on), or you can head over to the Don Juan Boulder and the Astrodomes, described below. Navigation becomes trickier, and casual explorers may want to turn back at this point.

For the Don Juan Boulder route, head for the left end of the larger South

Astrodome (the left rock). No trail here, so just scramble over rocks. The huge Don Juan Boulder should be clearly visible. From Don Juan, getting to the Astrodomes is straightforward but strenuous. Tiptoe through the cactus patch behind the behemoth boulder and scramble up the talus field below South Astrodome. It's worth going to the saddle between the two domes to have a look at the seemingly smaller North Astrodome. Its sheer 400-foot north face is the tallest vertical wall in the Park.

For the secret passage to Barker Dam, walk around to the back of the Don Juan Boulder and look for a ravine dense in foliage, to the south. Scramble over boulders, heading south to the foliage. Drop down into a ravine, where a small trail will weave through boulders and manzanita. After about 100 yards, the ravine bends sharply to the right. Tiptoe through a bit of beavertail cactus and exit the tight canyon, following a watercourse down a granite dome. (On the left is the Valhalla Dome; it is possible to ascend it at this point. See page 101.) Continue along the watercourse, turn left (S) at a wash, and follow the wash to the far side of Barker Dam Lake. Cross the lake, turn right, and walk the Barker Dam Loop Trail in reverse to reach the Barker Dam parking lot. Once in the lot, take the trail on the right side of the restrooms, which leads back to the Wonderland South parking lot (2.25 miles total for this variation).

HIKE

Garret's Arch, Elephant Arches - #17

Total distance: 4 miles (5 miles for both)
Physical difficulty: 2
Technical difficulty: 2
Navigating: 5
Trail type: climber trails/cross country

Garret's Arch and Elephant Arches are the most difficult locations to find in this book, especially Elephant Arches. Wandering this deep into the Wonderland should only be attempted by those with considerable experience in navigating rocky terrain, and preferably those already familiar with this part of the Wonderland.

Those who do brave the labyrinth of granite will be rewarded with the finest wilderness experience that Joshua Tree can offer. It's hard to believe that one can reach such a remote place, and feel so cut-off from the rest of the world, by hiking only 2 miles from a parking lot. The solitude here can be so intense that city-slickers may find their ears ringing from the silence. The trail picks up where the Wonderland South Valley trail leaves off, in the heart of the Wonderland, wandering through more steep-walled

The Red Obelisk.

canyons lined with turbinella oak, piñon pine, and dotted with pools of precious desert water. Both trails end with a bit of hunting and exploring. Garret's Arch is said to be the largest natural arch in Joshua Tree. Debatable, but it certainly is among the finest, poised high up in the cliffs, with the blue sky visible behind it. By contrast, Elephant Arches looks unassuming on

Elephant Arches.

approach. It's not until closer inspection that one notices there are actually three closely spaced arches, and the reason for the name becomes clear.

Details: See Wonderland of Rocks South Valley trail, page 108, for the beginning of this hike. Upon entering the South Valley, continue straight ahead for another 0.4 miles, following the wash and the intermittent trail that meanders back and forth, heading for a gap in the granite formations. At the gap the wash becomes deep and sandy, and the granite spires and domes tower overhead. The three-spired formation on the right is called the Freak Brothers Dome.

For Garret's Arch: Once in the gap, pass through a deep canyon on the right (E). The obvious path to the canyon is to beeline through a notch between Freak Brothers Dome and a small rock pile, but this path is tedious and not recommended. Instead, continue ahead (N) in the main wash for another 100 yards before turning right, traveling over some rocks to a small drainage that backtracks a bit to reach the canyon's entrance. It should be an easy walk into the canyon at this point. Continue through the verdant canyon, passing a thin granite spire known as the Red Obelisk. Once through the canyon, a broad valley opens up. Take a visual bearing here; if you were to continue in a straight line from the canyon through the valley to the other side, you would land below Garret's Arch. Head through the valley for approximately 500 yards to the rocks on the other side. At this point a bit of hunting around is required to locate the arch, which is found behind a bulbous chunk of granite perched high on a rocky formation.

For Elephant Arches: From the gap mentioned above, continue ahead (N) as the wash enters a long, flat valley lined with rock formations. Walk for another 0.4 miles to where a somewhat prominent drainage opens up on the right (E). Take the wash into a side canyon for 300 yards, then cut left (N), heading over a rocky notch, to a second small and very bushy canyon heading east/west. Turn right (E) and either walk a faint game trail through the middle of the bushy canyon, or walk alongside the canyon on the rocks above for another 150 yards. The small canyon will open up at a small alcove, where the Elephant Arches are located, almost at ground level.

For either arch, return as you came.

Garret's Arch.

CHAPTER 4
SOUTH CENTRAL
JOSHUA TREE

Watching the eons go by: A juniper at Keys View overlooks the lights of Coachella Valley during a late summer thunderstorm.

South Central Joshua Tree is the southern end of the popular Central Valley, where Park Boulevard loops around the southern end of the valley, traverses the base of Ryan Mountain, then exits the valley at Sheep Pass. There are many points of interest along this route. At Cap Rock, visitors can find a pleasant nature trail that is wheelchair-friendly. The trail weaves through rocks as it loops around a small rock formation, with informative signs along the way. A spur road at Cap Rock, Keys View Road, leads up into Joshua Tree high country, where mule deer and bighorn sheep roam, and forests of juniper take over the view. Keys View Road passes by one of Joshua Tree's best-preserved mining operations, the Lost Horse Mine. You won't be snapping any photos of the mine from the car, though, as it's a 2-mile walk uphill to reach the site! The road eventually ends at Keys View, which sits on the southern edge of the Park's high plateau. Below you is the large graben of Coachella Valley, with the Santa Rosa mountain chain and the Salton Sea beyond. Beyond the Keys View spur, Park Boulevard bends to the east and then again back north, passing one of the smaller campgrounds in the Park, Ryan Campground. Sitting next to the campground is the precariously balanced Headstone Rock, and just beyond that, the photogenic Ryan Ranch ruin. From Ryan Ranch, the road travels along the mighty Ryan Mountain and its iconic rock formations that form the backdrop of central Joshua Tree. One of the rock formations hides a cool little chasm you can walk into; some call it the Hall of Horrors, others, the Chasm of Doom. Before exiting over Sheep Pass, the road passes by another Park highlight, the Ryan Mountain Summit Trail. This moderately strenuous hike leads to the top of Ryan Mountain, which offers stunning 360-degree views of the entire Joshua Tree plateau. On a clear day it's possible to see 100 miles in every direction.

CAP ROCK

The area's name comes from a large capstone sitting atop the largest rock formation, jutting out like the brim of a baseball cap. Picnic tables, barbeques, and a wheelchair-accessible restroom can be found at the base of the rock. The area is popular with climbers; climbing classes are held here, so its not uncommon to see them festooning the cliffs and boulders around the parking lot. A nice paved nature trail circles a nearby formation, weaving

The "cap" on Cap Rock.

through rock and boulders, with information signs describing local plants. The trail is wheelchair accessible.

One other interesting thing to check out while you are here: On the northwest corner of the Cap Rock formation is a truly massive boulder, one of the largest in the Park, rivaled only by the Don Juan Boulder in the Wonderlandand. Near the base of this boulder is the shrine to the late musician Gram Parsons (see page 117).

Cap Rock is located just off of Park Boulevard, approximately 1.7 miles south of Intersection Rock. Turn south on Keys View Road, then left into the parking lot just after the bend. Cap Rock is the large formation on the left.

SOUTH CENTRAL JOSHUA TREE

N

to Central
Joshua Tree/
Intersection
Rock

Hall of
Horrors

parking

parking

Sheep Pass
Group
Campground

Saddle
Rock

21

18

Cap
Rock
Nature
Trail

parking

Ryan
Ranch

Ryan
Campground

Ryan
Mountain

22

parking
1.8 miles

Johnny Lang
grave

2.4 miles

20

Queen Valley
Link-Up

Lost
Pencil

Queen
Valley

parking

Lost
Horse
Mine Trail

19

Lost Horse Mine

Keys View

parking

old chimney

Park Boulevard

Park Boulevard

Keys View Road

Keys's View Road

Keys's Viking Trail

California Riding and Hiking Trail

California Hiking Trail

HIKE

Cap Rock Nature Trail - #18

Total distance: 0.5 miles
Physical difficulty: 1
Technical difficulty: 1

Navagating: 1
Trail type: paved/wheelchair-accessible

The Cap Rock Nature Trail is a paved, wheelchair-accessible loop trail. It exits from the parking lot and crosses open desert to a nearby rocky formation, where it loops around and joins back up near its starting point. Informative signs describe the flora found along the path, including information about the plants' roles in the ecosystem and how Native Americans utilized them. Around the back of the formation, the trail weaves through large boulders and a rocky corridor, with bench seats scattered here and there along the path. An interesting side journey circles the main Cap Rock formation past one of the largest boulders in the Park. Called Beaver Boulder, the rock appears as if it rolled out of a bowl from the top of Cap Rock. Near the base is the unofficial "Gram Parsons Memorial" (see sidestory opposite). Diehard fans have continued

to erect shrines here since 1973. The Park Service periodically removes the items and erases painted tributes.

Details: The trail starts roughly in the middle of the east side of the parking lot. Locate a long boulder at the front of the lot; the trail starts just to the right of this, by the restroom behind the boulder. Duck under the low-hanging Joshua tree and follow the paved path as it bends to the right. Take the right fork and continue following the trail as it slowly wraps around the formation. Eventually the trail will squeeze between two large boulders. Benches can be found in this area. Continue wrapping around to the left, then wind through a rocky corridor, eventually returning to the Cap Rock parking lot. For the side trek to the Memorial: Head to the restroom but continue ahead, walking along the base of the formation. Scant trails

116

Cap Rock and neighboring Yablonski Rock. Echo Rock is the large dome in the distance, on the right.

will bend around to the left, circling the base of the formation. Look for the massive boulder sitting on the ground on the north tip of the formation. Walk around the front of the boulder to large flakes that have exfoliated off the rock. The Gram Parsons Memorial is at the far right side of the flakes. From there, a faint trail continues around the formation and back to the parking lot.

Gram Parsons Memorial:
Gram Parsons was a musician and songwriter in the 1960s and early 1970s. He is best known for his work with The Byrds, The Flying Burrito Brothers, and the International Submarine Band. In the late '60s, Gram took an affinity to Joshua Tree (then a Monument) and spent much of his free time here. Late one evening, Gram was found slumped over in a local hotel, unresponsive from a drug overdose. He was transported to Hi Desert Memorial Hospital, where he died early the next morning.

Temporary artwork at the Gram Parsons Memorial.

As authorities were in the process of shipping Parsons' body back to his family in Louisiana, followers pinched the casket at the Los Angeles International Airport, bringing it back to Joshua Tree, where, in accord with Parsons' wishes they cremated him, pouring five gallons of gasoline into the open casket and setting the whole thing ablaze beneath the massive Beaver Boulder at Cap Rock. For many years after, a concrete slab sat beneath the boulder memorializing the event; this slab has recently been moved to the hotel where his body was first discovered. That hasn't stopped his fans from paying their respects at the boulder, though, as ad-hoc shrines continue to pop up at the site.

JOHNNY LANG AND THE LOST HORSE MINE

Like a window into the past, this site contains a very well preserved mining operation from the richest gold strike in the Park, the Lost Horse Mine. Machinery, sealed shafts (some 600 feet deep!), and ravaged land abound on this nonetheless beautiful ridgeline. Pop over the small hill behind the mine and be rewarded with unique views of Geology Tour Road and the cinder cone known as Malapia Hill.

This tale begins with a young Johnny Lang. At the close of the 1800s, Lang found himself temporarily shacked up at the Piñon Well mining camp, located on the lower flanks of Geology Tour Road. One day, Lang became separated from his horse. He tracked the beast into a neighboring valley, eventually wandering into the McHaney camp. There, the shifty gang leader Jim McHaney explained to him that his horse was "no longer lost," and to get with his own kind! Outnumbered and outgunned, Lang beat feet, ending up at Witch Spring (later to become the Ryan Ranch), where he met up with a one Frank Diebold. Diebold, who had his own problems with the McHaney gang, confided in Lang that he had recently discovered a rich gold prospect, but could not reach the site

to mark it due to the McHaney gang roaming over the area. Lang bought the prospect from Diebold outright for $1000, McHaney troubles and all. Lang tried several times to get out to his new prospect and to mark it, but every time he entered the valley, the McHaney gang would run him off. Eventually Lang brought in partners, and in 1893 developed the claim into a full-blown mining operation.

In the years following, the operation became wildly successful, yielding over 9000 troy ounces of gold. Lang continued to work at the mine during these years, taking on the position of night-shift supervisor. As time went on, the night shift began to report less amalgam than the day shift. Noticing this, partner Jep Ryan ordered one of his men to spy on the night shift, where he found Lang himself pocketing the precious treasure. Ryan confronted Lang with an ultimatum: sell his share or go to jail! Lang sold for $12,000. After that, Johnny Lang retreated to a nearby canyon in the vicinity of Quail Springs.

The mine continued to prosper for several more years until a fault was encountered and the vein disappeared. Many years later, a tired

Structure at the Lost Horse Mine.

and old Johnny Lang moved back in at the abandoned mining site, the place of his heyday. On January 25, 1925, Bill Keys found a note tacked to the door of Lang's shack: "Gone to town for food, be back soon." Lang never returned. Months later, his partially mummified remains were discovered near the road, still wrapped in a thin canvas sleeping bag and with nothing more than a piece of bacon and a small sack of flour for the journey.

HIKE

Lost Horse Mine Trail - #19

Total distance: 4 miles (round trip)
Physical difficulty: 3
Technical difficulty: 1
Navagating: 1
Trail type: official trail/old road

This trail follows an old road that leads up to the mine. The road traverses prime Joshua Tree highland wilderness as it winds and and weaves through the hills that separate central Joshua Tree and the valley of Geology Tour Road. Typically, this terrain would be dense with piñon pine, juniper, and Joshua trees, but most of the vegetation in the hills surrounding the mine was cut down and used as fuel to power the various steam engines at the site. The land is healing, albeit very slowly, with many young Joshua trees and junipers now dotting the hillsides.

Not much remains of the camp other than the stone foundations and scattered junk. The 10-stamp mill, however, is in excellent condition, as is other mechanized equipment surrounding the mine. A string of braided trails behind the mine leads up to a nice vantage point on the hilltop, with excellent views of the lower half of Geology Tour Road, including Malapia Hill, a thimble of rock called the Pencil, and many other rock formations. There is an extension to this trail that leads past several more mines, with the scant remains of several structures (including part of a log house), down to flat ground, and finally back to the parking lot. This extension is only recommended for the adventurous, though, as the road/trails are vague, and there are several dangerous unsealed mines in the area.

Also worth mentioning is an alternate start that travels up a verdant canyon, trudging through deep sand and over rocky cascades as it winds past mature piñon pines and towering nolinas,

Top: Mining equipment at the Lost Horse Mine.
Below: Johnny Lang's gravestone.

leading on to its point of origin at the mine camp above. Some people call this the Nolina Canyon Trail. It is a must to check out in the late spring, when the nolinas shoot out their huge flower stalks to tower over the wash.

Finally, on a quiet stretch of Keys View Road near the turnoff to the mine, there rests a small gravesite and headstone, the final resting place for a lifelong-resident of Joshua Tree— Johnny Lang.

(continue on next page)

119

(Lost Horse Mine Trail, continued)

Details: Take Keys View Road past Cap Rock, heading south for approximately 2.5 miles, to a junction with a dirt road on the left. Turn left and follow the road to the parking lot. Restrooms can be found here. Once on foot, take the clearly marked road/trail that leaves the lot on its east side. The rugged road ascends into the hills, veering to the right (S) and winding through the rolling terrain to the mine site. The road first leads through the camp, passing the crumbling foundations, before ending at the mine. Trails behind the 10-stamp mill lead to the vantage point.

For the alternate start, head into the large, sandy wash that parallels the road/trail to the right. Continue up the wash (E) in its main channel, as it veers to the right (S), gradually becoming smaller. The wash will eventually fizzle out as it joins with the main road/trail, just before the mine.

For Johnny Lang's gravestone, park on Keys View Road at the junction with the dirt road that leads to the Lost Horse Mine parking lot. From there, walk back along Keys View Road, heading north, on the opposite side of the road from the dirt road. After about 40 yards, look for the headstone and small grave ring on the desert floor. The site is not officially marked, so it is easily overlooked.

Stunning vistas at Keys View.

KEYS VIEW

Keys View is an excellent lookout point sitting on the edge of the uplifted plateau of Joshua Tree National Park. Beyond the edge is the sinking graben of Coachella Valley. At this point, visitors are virtually standing on the bow of the North American Continental Plate. Wave goodbye as the Pacific Plate on the opposite side of the valley slowly tears away and heads north, with the mighty San Andreas Fault visibly marking the boundary in the baking earth below the lookout. The vantage point also offers panoramic views of Mount San Jacinto and the Santa Rosa Mountains. On a clear day you can see the Salton Sea and perhaps even as far as Mexico. Bighorn sheep are frequently spotted here.

Reportedly, Bill Keys built the original road out to the precipice, to serve a mine he had down in the ravines below the lookout. Nothing remains of the mine, named the Secret Mine, save for a hole in the earth. One more thing to note: it is often very windy at Keys View, especially at the upper vantage point, so, hold on to your hat!

To get to Keys View, simply drive Keys View Road to its end at the viewpoint. A short but steep concrete path leads to a vantage point on the hilltop in front of the parking area. There is also a limited vantage point at the parking lot, as well as restrooms. A wheelchair-accessible lookout and parking can be found roughly 1/4 mile before the end loop.

Joshua trees in the mist, Keys View.

RYAN CAMPGROUND

This small campground is found in the southeast corner of Joshua Tree's Central Valley, nestled at the base of Ryan Mountain. This seasonal campground has 30 sites scattered about beneath two rocky formations. There are several areas of interest within easy walking distance of the campground. The picturesque Ryan Ranch ruin is a short 1/4-mile walk, and you will pass several other unusual sights enroute, including the gravity-defying Headstone Rock. And for those looking to go on a long walk, there's the Queen Valley Link-Up.

The turnoff for the campground is located on Park Boulevard, 2.2 miles southeast of Intersection Rock (0.6 miles east of Keys View Road). Turn south onto a dirt road that leads into the campground. Once at the campground, an information board and fee kiosk can be found on the right. The dirt road becomes a one-way loop at this point. Aside from campsites, there are also several day-use parking turnouts as well as an equestrian parking area for the California Riding and Hiking Trail.

The picturesque Headstone Rock, near Ryan Campground.

The Ryan Ranch ruin with a cloudscape background.

THE RYAN RANCH RUIN

was originally built and owned by Lost Horse Mine partners Thomas and Jep Ryan in the late 1880s. The brothers made a homestead claim here to secure water from a spring at the location, to be used at the Lost Horse Mine. A pipeline ran from the spring, called Witch Spring, all the way out to the mine some 8 miles away. (Sections of the pileline can still be seen along the Queen Valley link-up trail.) The main structure caught fire and burned down in 1978. Several other small structures can be found scattered around the ranch, as well as day-to-day objects and junk from the life of 1800s gold miners.

The trail leading out to the ruin has several points of interest. Nearby, a large teetering block called Headstone Rock can be seen at the top of a rocky formation. Needless to say, it is very popular with rock climbers. In a rocky alcove near the trail is a long-abandoned Native American camp. Several matates and the odd pottery shard are all that remain here. Finally, just outside the ranch entry gate (what's left of it) is a small graveyard from the mining era. It takes a discerning eye to spot the several overgrown, rock-outlined graves on the ground at the back of the small rocky formation to the right of the trail. Faint markings on the nearby boulders give scant clues about the yard's occupants.

To get to the ruin from the campground, take one of several trails on the north side of the camp loop. The trails converge and head north to the ruin, approximately 1/4 mile away. If you're not camping here, park at the turnout on Park Boulevard, just north of the road into Ryan Campground (2.2 miles SE of Intersection Rock, or 0.6 miles east of Keys View Road). The turnout has restrooms and an information board. Take the obvious trail for approximately 1/3 mile to the ruin.

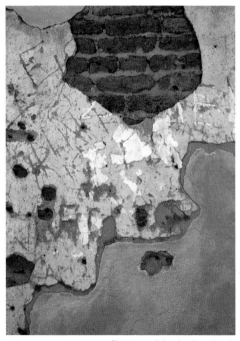
Layers of history: wall detail at Ryan Ranch.

Top: Barbed wire at the Ryan Ranch.
Middle: Rock formation framed by Ryan Ranch walls.
Bottom: Shadowplay on the walls at the Ryan Ranch.

Photography notes:
The Ryan Ranch Ruin is a photogenic structure! Situated on the hillside at the far eastern end of Joshua Tree's Central Valley, the ruin's locale is prime for catching that sought-after late-afternoon light. Centrally located and sitting slightly elevated on a mound, the main structure offers 360 degrees of compositional possibilities. The ruin's sinuous, organic curves blend perfectly with the surrounding landscape; by contrast, its monolithic walls stand hard-edged and geometric, statuesque in feel. A cottonwood snag growing next to the ruin seems to mimic the bends and curves of the structure's walls, accentuating its organic nature. The ranch is also a great place to be at sunset!

HIKE

Queen Valley Link-Up - #20

Total distance: 6 miles (round trip)
Physical difficulty: 2
Technical difficulty: 1

Navagating: 1
Trail type: official

The Queen Valley Link-Up is actually just a section of the much longer California Riding and Hiking Trail (see page 29). The trail—designated for hiking and equestrian use—follows an old mine road leading through a gap south of Ryan Mountain, eventually heading past several prospects and on into lower Queen Valley. Remnants of the old Lost Horse water pipeline can be seen along the trail. The line ran from Witch Spring on the Ryan Ranch to the Lost Horse Mine, some 8 miles distant. Once in Queen Valley, hikers have the option of exploring the remote rock formations that dot the wide-open valley all the way to Geology Tour Road, 2 miles across the desert floor. Faint signs of Native American life can be found scattered around at the base of several of the rock piles. One interesting rock, called the Lost Pencil, balances precariously on the edge of a cliff, the spitting image of Headstone Rock at Ryan Campground.

Details: Parking can be found at the east end of the Ryan Campground loop; there is also an equestrian parking area on the right just past the entrance kiosk. A large road/trail leaves the parking turnout at the east end of the loop. Take the trail as it heads gently up the valley and into a gap in the hills south of Ryan Mountain. Continue straight on (E) for about 2 miles. Eventually the trail will exit the gap, crossing into the rugged, dark-colored hills. Follow the winding road to several small mine pits. To continue on to the rock formations, follow the main wash out into the open desert. From there, just cut across the open desert (with no trails) to the rock piles. The Lost Pencil is located to the southeast, and should be visible (albeit well-camouflaged) from the mines at the end of the road/trail.

THE HALL OF HORRORS AREA

Another area that is popular with rock climbers, this one comprised of three long rock formations. A fourth rock dome loiters further out in the desert beyond. Small trails braid throughout the rocks in every direction. If you have kids, or are a kid at heart, the many boulders, crevices, and corridors at the base of the formations are great for exploring. One corridor runs 100 feet deep and just as long, straight into a rocky formation. The corridor, sometimes called The "Real" Hall of Horrors, is worth a closer look!

Just across the way from the parking lot, jutting out of the side of Ryan Mountain, is the massive Saddle Rock, the largest dome in Joshua Tree. A well-trodden climber trail leads straight to the base, where a pleasant alcove can be found with tall piñon pines and delicate flora growing around a seep. A massive shard of granite broke off from the dome, landing at its base and forming an interesting cave. Rock climbers line up to climb one of the most popular, and longest, routes in the Park, "Walk On the Wild Side," which ascends the main face of Saddle Rock.

The Hall of Horrors parking lot is located 3 miles east of Intersection Rock, and 0.75 miles from Sheep Pass. The large lot is on the west side of the road, just across from the massive Saddle Rock on the side of Ryan Mountain. Restrooms can be found here.

Cottonwood snag and the Ryan Ranch ruin at sundown.

The real Hall of Horrors.

THE "REAL" HALL OF HORRORS

This thin, deep corridor—about 100 feet deep, 100 feet long, and 6 to 8 feet wide—is a crack in the granite dome that has opened up over the ages. The floor is level and filled with inviting sand. The Hall is a favorite for digeridoo and tambourine jam sessions, and gauging by the occasional candle wax dripping from various places in the back of the corridor, the odd midnight pow-wow! Note that it requires a small amount of rock hopping to enter the Hall.

Details: Take the trail that starts just left of the restroom, heading off north, around the right side of the long rock formation in front of the parking lot. Once around the right end of the formation, turn left and follow a sandy wash that goes between the two rocks. The Hall of Horrors is on the far left end of the formation on the right side of the wash. Exit the wash and head for the left end of the rock formation. Look for a small alcove on the formation's end and walk into it. Scramble up rocks at the back of the alcove and look for the somewhat hidden entrance to the hall. Drop down 10 feet to reach the floor.

HIKE

Saddle Rock - #21

Total distance: 0.75 miles (round trip)
Physical difficulty: 1
Technical difficulty: 1
Navagating: 1
Trail type: marked climber trail

This short trek takes advantage of one of the many climber's trails that can be found throughout the Park. The trail leads up the steepening pediment at the base

The gargantuan Saddle Rock.

of Ryan Mountain, weaving up washes and over rolling hills to reach the base of Saddle Rock. There is a distinctive, darker-colored rock lying around in the area, unlike the lighter granite typically found in Joshua Tree. This ancient (1.8-billion-year-old) rock is the Pinto Gneiss.

Saddle Rock, named for its saddle shape, may be the largest dome in the Park. Its west face is over 400 feet tall, certainly the biggest cliff in Joshua Tree. No doubt much of the dome remains hidden inside of the mountain. Several of the Park's most sought-after rock climbs are located on the dome's west face, and climbers can usually be found swinging all over the rock. One route in particular, "Walk On the Wild Side," is so popular that it tends to get backed up with a line of climbers waiting to have a go. The route was first ascended in 1970.

Details: In the Hallof Horrors parking lot, just before the crossing, is an information board showing the locations of some of the rock-climbing routes on Saddle Rock. With a good pair of binoculars one can usually make out climbers on the routes shown on the board. To hike to the rock from the parking lot, carefully cross Park Boulevard and follow the marked trail east. The trail intermittently follows washes, ocassionally moving into the rolling hills. The main trail will end at the alcove at the base of Saddle Rock. Small climber trails continue around to the top of the rock on both sides. These trails can be steep and treacherous.

SHEEP PASS

Sheep Pass is a prominent notch in the north-south-trending Ryan Mountain chain, located just north of Ryan Mountain proper. The pass serves as the main corridor into Queen Valley. The area has two distinct locales: the Ryan Mountain trailhead, and the Sheep Pass Group Campground. The highlight of the area is the hike to the summit of Ryan Mountain.

The centerpiece of the Joshua Tree landscape, Ryan Mountain cleaves the Park's northwestern "high" plateau straight down the middle, the summit offering sweeping 360-degree views of Joshua Tree's most iconic areas: Queen Mountain, the Wonderland, Hidden Valley, Lost Horse Valley, Geology Tour Road, Jumbo Rocks, and Queen Valley. The summit lies 5,457 feet above sea level and the trail leading up to it gains 1000 feet of elevation in a brisk mile and a half.

Sheep Pass Group Campground is a reservation-only campground with minimum occupancy requirements (see Campground section on page 15). The grounds are in a great location, right on the edge of the expansive Queen Valley, with the mighty Ryan Mountain behind. Sites have rock piles to climb around on, and there are some great stony alcoves and washes around the east side of the hills. There is even a connecting trail to the Ryan Mountain Summit Trail, leaving from the west end of the campground.

To reach this area, drive Park Boulevard east past Intersection Rock, then follow it as it bends south and then curves back east (past Cap Rock) and finally north. The road then travels along the base of Ryan Mountain before bending east and heading over Sheep Pass. The road at this point is also referred to as Sheep Pass Road, but for the sake of simplicity, this guide just calls the road "Park Boulevard" for its entire stretch. The Ryan Mountain Trailhead parking will be the first encountered, followed by the campground entrance, about 0.75 miles further on the right.

HIKE

Ryan Mountain
Summit Trail - #22

Total distance: 3 miles (round trip)
Physical difficulty: 3
Technical difficulty: 1
Navagating: 1
Trail type: official

Ryan Mountain views.

Considered by some to be the best hike in Joshua Tree, this trail ascends the backbone of Ryan Mountain, leading to a lofty highpoint with a commanding view of the high desert. The hike starts out from rock piles at the northwest toe of the mountain. There, a Native American cave site can be found. The trail then heads steeply uphill on a rocky hillside. About halfway along the journey, the trail eases back as it weaves through rolling hillside on its way to the summit. Once on top of the mountain, the trail ends at a summit sign, located just below a rocky ridge where the true summit lies.

Looking west from the summit of Ryan Mountain.

The view from the summit is stunning, a birds-eye view of the entire Central Joshua Tree area, as well as all of Queen Valley. On a clear day one can see 100 miles or more in every direction.

Details: Travel Park Boulevard northeast (toward Sheep Pass) several miles past the Hall of Horrors parking area, looking for another large lot on the right. A trailhead marks the route. The well-worn trail travels right of the rock formations and then traverses diagonally up the mountainside toward Saddle Rock.

Looking into the Geology Tour Road area from the summit of Ryan Mountain.

CHAPTER 5

QUEEN VALLEY

Queen Valley is a long north-south-trending valley running parrallel to Joshua Tree's Central Valley and separated from it by the Ryan Mountain/Lost Horse mountain range. The lower portion of the valley drops steeply before intersecting with Pleasant Valley at its far southern end. Queen Valley boasts a wide variety of landscapes. At its northern boundary is Queen Mountain. The mountain and the plains below it are dense in juniper, piñon pine, and turbinella oak. At its northeastern perimeter, the valley—more like the edge of a plateau at this point—drops away, with deep canyons radiating out into the eroded landscape below. The middle of the valley, where Park Boulevard cuts through, is so flat you'd swear you could see the curvature of the earth across it! Joshua tree forests cover the open plains as far as the eye can see. On the lower flanks of Queen Valley, the lay of the land changes once again.

(continue)

Wide-open spaces in Queen Valley, with Jumbo Rocks in the distance.

23
Queen
Mountain

parking
Upper Queen
Valley

parking

25
Desert
Queen
Mine

old
parking

parking

Queen Valley Road
Bighorn Pass Road
Park Boulevard

Sheep Pass
Campground

Old Dell Road

Queen

Desert Queen Mine Road

parking

Jumbo Rocks
Campground

parking
1.5 miles

Geology Tour Road

Riding and H

N

QUEEN
VALLEY

Malapia
Hill

27
parking
4.6 miles

to Pleasant
Valley

Bighorn Pass Ro

Park par
Barber
Pole

132

23 Queen Mountain

UPPER **Q**UEEN **V**ALLEY

N

Pine City

24

Desert Queen Mine

25

Backcountry Board

parking

26 Eagle Cliffs Mine

alley Road

Desert Queen Mine Road

Split Rock Parking

North Entrance (Chapter 6)

parley Rd

parking

(continued)

Sand is much more prevalent on this side, and granite outcroppings, like those of central Joshua Tree, dot the landscape.

Back in the northern part of Queen Mountain, several pleasant walks lead out across the verdant high country. Another of the Park's more interesting mining operations can also be found in this area: Desert Queen Mine. This mine has several ruins, machinery, and other mining-related objects scattered about. The remains of shelters and other claims can be found hidden in cubbies and under rocks. One secluded shelter is fascinatingly well-preserved.

Traveling straight through the wide-open plain of middle Queen Valley is Park Boulevard. This area has some beautiful Joshua tree forests, and several very interesting trees can be observed right off the road. Look for a turnout on the north side of the road, with a very large Joshua tree next to it. This is Elmer's Tree. A large section of the tree fell in recent years, but what remains is still impressive. Across the road from Elmer's Tree is perhaps the most unusual tree in the Park. Called the Barber Pole, this tall Joshua tree is a single trunk for the first 30 feet. It only recently sprouted branches. Near the junction with Geology Tour Road is a site where a past wildfire that swept through the area. Like some long-extinct beasts, the bleached and dessicated remains of fallen Joshua trees lie scattered across the desert floor, stark yet strangely beatiful.

In the lower southern region of Queen Valley lies a dark, ominous mound, Malapia Hill, its flanks coated in dark lava flows. A short and moderately strenuous hike leads to the summit of this dormant volcano, where interesting columnar-jointed basalt can be observed. Dotting the desert near Malapia Hill are many granite rock piles concealing numerous Native American sites, one of which is easily discovered at the final stop on Geology Tour Road, Squaw Tank. This area also has some beautifully eroded rock.

Last light of the day falls on Queen Mountain.

HIKE

Queen Mountain - #23

Total distance: 4 miles (round trip to summit)
Physical difficulty: 5 (summit)
Technical difficulty: 4 (summit)
Navagating: 5 (summit)
Trail type: dirt road, climber trail, rock scrambling to the summit

View from the summit of Queen Mountain.

Queen Mountain is a rocky and steep mountain forming the northern border of Queen Valley. Its rugged slopes, and the steep canyons and ridges behind it, guard some of the lushest and most beautiful landscapes in the Park. There are climber trails that lead through these areas, but they are difficult to describe and difficult to follow—beware! There is, however, a walk that travels a well-worn mine road to, and along, the base of the mountain. This 1-mile jaunt crosses a colorful mineralized desert floor, moving through desert forests of yucca, creosote, piñon pine, scrub oak, and a wide variety of native succulents, on its way to the mountain base. The road ends at an old parking lot at the edge of the mountain. For those who wish to go further, a small climber trail continues along the base of the mountain, eventually ascending a prominent gully to a flat near the summit. From there, brutal slogging up rocky gullies leads to the true summit at 5687 feet above sea level. But the view, as would be expected, is fantastic!

Details: From Park Boulevard (6 miles east of Intersection Rock or 1 mile west of Jumbo Rocks Campground), take a dirt road that leads north. After approximately 1/4 mile you reach a fork; go right (the left fork leads to the Barker Dam area). A bit futher along there will be an intersection; continue straight on toward the mountain. After another mile the dirt road will dead-end at the small O'Dell parking loop. The old road actually continues on to the base of the mountain, but it is blocked off to vehicle travel.

Continue on foot. The badly eroded road travels north over a pass in a small hill, then on across the desert to the base of the mountain, a mile distant. Once at the mountain, the road will bend to the right (E) and ascend slightly to reach the old parking lot. Casual hikers might want to stop here, as trail finding becomes much more difficult ahead! Take a small trail that exits the east side of the dirt loop and heads along the base of the mountain. Take care to locate both sides of the trail at the sandy wash crossing, as it is easy to lose track of it in this spot (even worse on the return!). After the wash, the trail will begin to veer uphill, eventually joining with a prominent gully. Once in the gully the trail becomes quite steep and rugged, ascending the first 1000 vertical feet of the mountain in just a few hundred yards. At the top of the gully, a high plateau is gained. From this point on, it's no man's land! The pointy summit is a wicked scramble up the obvious rocky gully, fraught with unstable boulders and dense vegetation.

Phantom light. A late summer thunderstorm in Queen Valley.

Granite sphere, near the Desert Queen Mine.

DESERT QUEEN MINE AREA

This area is located on the northeast corner of Queen Valley, sitting on the edge of a high plateau of sorts. The deeply incised valleys that drop away to the north and east feature some extended hikes. On the edge of one of the deepest valleys is Desert Queen Mine. An easy walk out to the ridge gives a bird's-eye view of the operation as well as the rock-and-mortar remains of a structure. A steep road leading down into the canyon offers a closer inspection of the machinery and sealed mine entrances, as well as access to the gorgeous canyon itself. Hidden among the rocks are several shelters, one of which, the Eagle Mine house, is a fascinating window into the hardscrabble life of a desert prospector. The home is built into a rock crevice, complete with crates, a chiminea, a stove, and pots and pans still hanging on the wall! The site so well hidden, however, that it is nearly impossible to find.

Details: Just across Park Boulevard from Geology Tour Road is a dirt road leading north. Take this dirt road for approximately 1 mile to where it dead-ends in the Desert Queen Mine parking lot. Restrooms can be found here. There is also a Backcountry Board with a map detailing day-use boundaries and describing Pine City. This board is at the north end of the parking. The trail leading out to Desert Queen Mine can be found to the right of the restroom.

 **HIKE**

Pine City - #24

Total distance: 3 miles (round trip)
Physical difficulty: 2
Technical difficulty: 1

Navigating: 1
Trail type: official/dirt road

This pleasant walk across the high desert of Joshua Tree follows an old mine road to a canyon ridge. The name is a bit misleading as there is no "city," or even scant evidence of one. It's the journey, and not so much the destination, that makes this hike enjoyable. The road travels rocky ground alongside a verdant wash with dark sand. An abundance of minerals in this area gives the desert floor splashes of colors and sheens. A wide variety of flora adds to the scenery. Indeed, this is a prime locale for viewing wildflowers in the spring season.

Details: Take the large road/trail next to the Backcountry Board, heading north. It is also possible to walk the wash to the road's left. After a ways, the road will seemingly end at a sandy area with small rock formations. One can either take a small canyon between the formations, or go around left to where the road continues on northward. The road/trail will end at a rocky knoll sitting on the edge of a deep canyon. It's possible to continue on down the rugged hillside on a small trail leading into the wash in the middle of the canyon. From there, one could even continue down the wash to where it opens up near Park Boulevard and the North Entrance of the Park.

A piñon pine that once grew out of this granite crag now sits frozen in time. Located near the trail to Pine City.

HIKE

Desert Queen Mine - #25

Total distance: 1.5 miles (round trip)
Physical difficulty: 3
Technical difficulty: 1
Navigating: 1
Trail type: official/dirt road

Above: The Desert Queen Mine.
Middle: Old pulley on site.

This trek leads out to the edge of a large canyon, where the entire operation can be seen from a high vantage point. A bit of backtracking leads to the remains of a stone structure, and the steep, eroded road that weaves down into the canyon. The road down offers a great view of the mine on the opposite side of the canyon wall. Several faint side roads lead off to other small stone structures in a nearby canyon. The wash at the base of the large canyon is filled with deep sand, turbinella oak, and a few large boulders. Discarded mining equipment and junk can be found strewn all up and down the wash.

Interesting side hikes can be taken both upstream and downstream. Heading upstream will lead through more large boulders and oak trees before opening up in a broader canyon; going downstream will lead deeper into the large canyon as it bends east and cuts a path to the large valley near the North Entrance.

Back at the mine, take the road located on the opposite side of the wash back uphill to reach the mine itself. A few well-worn pieces of equipment can be seen alongside the road. The mine pits all lie near the summit and all are grated off for safety. Good thing, because the summit is riddled with vertical shafts!

140

The office/bunkhouse, located several hundred yards from the parking lot, before the old road descends into the canyon.

Details: From the parking lot, take the road/trail on the east side of the lot, to the right of the restroom. This road travels mostly flat ground for approximately 500 yards, first to the ruin and road leading down into the canyon, then to the vantage point 100 yards further. Take the road that travels downhill from the ruin to reach the wash and mines on the opposite side of the hill. The severely eroded road travels down the hillside to the bottom of the canyon, maybe 1/3 mile distant. Cross the sandy wash at the canyon's base, then travel back uphill for another 300 yards to the mine pits and the summit.

Sidestory: Desert Queen Mine Folly

In 1879, two brothers, Bill and Jim McHaney, came into ownership of what was to become the Desert Queen Ranch, starting a successful (and suspect) cattle operation in the high desert of Joshua Tree. The McHaney Gang, including the likes of Ike Chestnut, George Myers, Charley Martin, and the Button brothers, Willie and Charlie, were notorious for "acquiring" cattle and horses, temporarily hiding them in the rocks of Hidden Valley and other locations around Joshua Tree. In one incident of classic McHaney mayhem, Jim caught wind of a rather rich piece of ore in the possession of a lone prospector working at the Lost Horse Mine (see Johnny Lang and the Lost Horse Mine, page 118). McHaney reportedly ordered his men to follow the prospector, Frank Diebold, to find the location of his secret strike. On April 5, 1894, Frank Diebold was reported dead, the result of two gunshot wounds inflicted by Charley Martin. Diebold had allegedly attempted to jump a claim site that the McHaneys "found" the day before: the Desert Queen Mine.

The McHaneys made a tidy profit during the short period that they were in possession of the Desert Queen Mine, reportedly up to $40,000 dollars (a lot in the 1890s), with Jim squandering his money on items such as diamond-encrusted hats, belts, and canes. Possession of the mine changed many times over the years, and in 1931, successful jeweler Fredrick Morton, under the influence of a shady fellow known only as Hapwell, bought the rights from Bill Keys (who had worked at the mine for many years). Hapwell, who was merely a mine cook, convinced Morton to finance his scheme. Purely by chance, Hapwell struck pay dirt, and of course hid the ore for himself. Once the pocket was exhausted, the tunnel was conveniently lost in an "accidental" collapse, thus ending the tribulations of the DQM.

141

HIKE

Eagle Cliffs Mine - #26

Total distance: 4 miles (round trip)
Physical difficulty: 3
Technical difficulty: 2
Navigating: 5
Trail type: unofficial trail/cross-country

Above: All the comforts of home at Eagle Cliffs Mine.
Below: The elegant chiminea found inside the cabin.

Eagle Cliffs Mine is a small claim located in the hills high above Desert Queen Mine. The mine is, for the most part, inconsequential; it's the small cabin built into the rocks nearby that makes this one of the most fascinating treasures in all of Joshua Tree National Park. Several walls remain, including one with a six-pane window, and the roof above is still intact. Gaps between the rocks were filled with rock-and-mortar walls, and a stone chimney was built into a crevice at the back of the cabin. Cupboards, shelving, crates, and a stove all remain intact; pots and cups lie around as if the cabin's occupants just left for the day.

The intact nature of the cabin's interior is a testament to the location's remoteness and to the discretion of past visitors who have chosen to leave the site as they found it. If you do actually find the place, please leave it as you found it too, so that it remains a treasure for future generations.

Details: From the hilltop above the Desert Queen Mine pits, as described in the Desert Queen Mine details, wander eastward past several sealed vertical shafts toward a tall boulder. A faint trail will become apparent, traveling left of the boulder. Take the trail, weaving through some rocks, and then on to the hill beyond. The trail will begin to contour the hill, bending to the left and heading north. Stay left at a junction that leads south into a high valley. The trail will reach a crest and bend to the right (E), then make a gradual descent into a rocky valley. Continue ahead as the trail slowly bends to

the south, passing through a rocky corridor and eventually switchbacking up the rocky south slope of the valley. Look for a small mine pit near the summit of the strenuous switchbacks. (If you are at a nice view from a mountaintop, you went too far!) Left of the mine pit is a very faint trail leading through boulders and into a small valley leading northeast. A rocky descent will turn into a noticable, but faint, trail. Look for a small pit that descends diagonally into the ground for about 25 feet. (Danger: Unsealed Mine! Entering old mines is very hazardous!) **Past the pit, the small valley opens up: Look for the somewhat camouflaged entrance and wall nestled in turbinella oak and boulders.**

View of lower Queen Valley including Geology Tour Road and Malapia Hill. Pleasant Valley is located beyond Malapia Hill.

GEOLOGY TOUR ROAD

Geology Tour Road is a dirt road that travels down into the lower, southern portion of Queen Valley. The name comes from a self-guided tour that the Park offers. On the "tour," the road passes by many granite rock piles, called inselbergs in geo-lingo, that are scattered across the broad valley floor. Many of these rock piles hide faint remnants of a once-thriving Native American community that lived here eons ago. Further down is the ominous Malapia Hill. This small cinder cone gets its dark shading from the lava flows running down its flanks. A short and strenuous hike leads up its east side. At the bottom of Queen Valley is one final rock pile, Squaw Tank, said to be the hub of the ancient community. Nothing remains of the community save for a small catchment, a few scattered matates, and the occasional pottery shard. There are some nicely eroded rocks to be viewed here, though.

Geology Tour Road does continue beyond the point of Squaw Tank, but it becomes a one-way, unmaintained road, and there are a few tricky spots for those without four-wheel drive. Right off the bat, drivers will hit some ruts and deep sand, as the road bends left and heads east. If you get past that point, the difficulties ease up for quite a way as the road travels along the base of the hill, eventually leading to a small mining operation, the Gold Coin Mine. There, a Backcountry Board can be found, as well as several large tanks left from the operation. This location sits on the edge of a broad, flat area known as Pleasant Valley. The valley is actually an ancient dry lake bed. In springtime this valley can become carpeted with wildflowers.

At the Gold Coin Mine, the road turns right (SW) and crosses the valley. This section is part of Berdoo Canyon Road (see page 149), which leads through a large canyon down into Coachella Valley and the Palm Springs area. Another junction on the right continues around the loop and back to Geology Tour Road proper.

143

Details: Geology Tour Road is a dirt road leading south off Park Boulevard, approximately 6.5 miles east of Intersection Rock, 15.5 miles from the West Entrance, or 9.75 miles from the North Entrance. Restrooms can be found here, as well as an information board and the kiosk for the tour pamphlets. The road is decent for passenger cars for the first 5.4 miles, when it becomes an unmaintained one-way loop road. The one-way loop portion of the road is another 6 miles; four-wheel drive is recommended!

HIKE

Malapia Hill - #27

Total distance: 1.25 miles (round trip)
Physical difficulty: 3
Technical difficulty: 2
Navigating: 2
Trail type: cross-country

As you descend Geology Tour Road through the lower flanks of Queen Valley, you'll encounter an unusually dark and lonesome hill, Malapai Hill. This beautiful reminder of Joshua Tree's violent geologic past is but one of several cinder cones within the park. The northwest and southeast sides of Malapia Hill both have large lava flows descending from the summit, and the southwest rim also exhibits fascinating columnar jointing. The hike itself is fairly mild, maybe a little more than 1-mile round trip, and with only 400 feet of gain to the summit.

Details: Drive south on Geology Tour Road for approximately 4.6 miles to a turnout on

Top: The ominous Malapia Hill with small granite inselbergs in the foreground.
Middle: Columnar jointing at the summit of Malapia Hill.

the right (watch for deep sand). Malapai Hill will be just west of the parking area. Head straight for the lava flow on the hillside, walking past several small rock piles enroute. Continue up the flow to the saddle in the summit. Go right (north) to the true summit, or head straight and slightly left to the ridge and small cliff to see the jointing. Beware: some of the column stacks can be loose and precariously balanced.

SQUAW TANK

At the end of the two-wheel section of Geology Tour Road is Squaw Tank. This is the last rock pile in this section of the Park. Here, highly eroded granite ourcroppings cover the landscape, creating a system of gullies, rivulets, and natural tanks. The area's ability to hold water attracted Native Americans, and this location is known to have had a rather large native community occupying it in the distant past. Nothing is left from this community, other than a few small grinding holes and the odd pottery shard.

The area later attracted cattle ranchers, who built a small dam to create a reservoir area that is maybe 25 feet long and 12 feet high: Squaw Tank. A short, marked trail leads roughly 150 yards through a wash to the tank.

Squaw Tank nestles among highly sculpted rocks.

Sidestory: The Enigma of Little William

Faintly etched into one of the plaster-covered bricks of Squaw Tank is the strange and mysterious rhyme of Little William. The etching is old and barely visible, nearly impossible to read, but determined history buffs have deciphered it. It goes something like this:

Little William age seven
Died and went to heaven
We can't always sometimes tell
But Little Willie might have went to hell

Well-hidden panel on Squaw Tank, with the Little William rhyme.

The origin of this etching is unknown, whether it was inscribed by a cattle rancher in the late 1800s/ early 1900s, or by someone at a later date. The Park Service currently views it as not being authentic from the time period. The etching does appear to be quite old though, and it kinda has that quirky old miner/frontiersman ring to it!

The expansive Pleasant Valley, as seen fron the Gold Coin Mine.

HIKE

Pleasant Valley - #28

Total distance: 1 mile (round trip)
Physical difficulty: 1
Technical difficulty: 1
Navigating: 1
Trail type: miner's road

Old cyanide tanks above the parking area at Pleasant Valley.

This pleasant hike follows an old mine road that cuts along the base of the Hexie Mountain Range and the edge of Pleasant Valley. Scant remnants from the Gold Coin Mine can be seen scattered in the hills above the road (danger: unsealed mine shafts in this area), making for interesting diversions along the hike. Pleasant Valley is the remnant of a dry lake from the last Ice Age. The mineralized soil at the surface creates a unique ecosystem, with only a few specialized varieties of flora being able to withstand the hardpan. Pleasant Valley is an excellent place for bird watching, and if you're lucky enough to be here when the spring flowers are in bloom, you're in for a spectacular show!

For those who can't get enough, the mine road continues on to several more points of interest: a stone house located at the mouth of Fried Liver Wash, and the Hexahedron Mine deep in the Hexie Mountains above Pleasant Valley. *(continue)*

147

(Pleasant Valley, continued)

Details: Just about the only unpleasant thing about this entire trek is the short section of unmantained road that has to be driven to reach the parking area—that, and the fact that drivers have to commit to the one-way road. (Some just reverse the short section after doing this hike, but you didn't hear that from me!) Drive Geology Tour Road for 5.4 miles to where it becomes a one-way loop road. Punch it over the ruts! The road quickly bends left (E) and heads gently downhill, starting out in thick sand and becoming more solid on the way down. After another mile or so, the valley floor will be reached and then the parking area. Look for the Backcountry Board and the large cyanide tanks above. Park at the board and follow the obvious road/trail east. Continue along the road, or head out onto the valley floor.

As inviting as the back nine at Indian Wells Golf Resort, Pleasant Valley lives up to its name.

4X4 TRAIL

Berdoo Canyon

Total distance: 17 miles (from Squaw Tank)
Difficulties: easy/moderate, deep sand with a short section of rock crawling
Navigating: 2

The Berdoo Canyon Road is a popular 4x4 trail traveling through a massive drainage that leads out of the Park and into the Coachella Valley/Palm Springs area. The road was originally an old teamsters route. The majority of it is easy travel in sandy washes. There is one section, though, that offers some good (and mandatory) rock crawling, where the wash pinches down to a tight canyon choked with boulders. Near the bottom the drainage becomes a massive wash, where many short, sandy, steep, and rutted hills can be found to play on.

The bottom of the drainage, where it opens up into Coachella Valley, is unfortunately an environmental disaster-zone. There was at one time a large-scale operation at the mouth of the drainage, as evident from many structure foundations, graded terraces, and industrial garbage. These days, the place seems to be a popular refuse site, shooting range, and stolen-vehicle dumping grounds. Gang graffiti adds to the unsettling ambiance. The road/trail is very popular with local 4x4 tour companies, and it's not uncommon to see large groups out in this seemingly remote locale.

Details: Drive Geology Tour Road south to its end at Squaw Tank (5.4 miles), then continue on the one-way road as it bends east and and travels to the bottom of the valley. Turn right at the Pleasant Valley Backcountry Board and parking area. The road will head south across the dry lake bed, then gradually ascend the other side of the valley. Stay left at a junction about a mile from the Pleasant Valley parking; the right fork takes you around the Geology Tour loop. The terrain now goes from creosote desert, to Joshua trees, to juniper and piñon pine chapparel, and aside from occasional ruts, the road is pretty decent to drive on. Eventually the road will level off at the foot of some small hills. These little hills are actually the summit of the Little Berdoo Mountain Range, which rises 4000 feet above the Coachella Valley on the range's south side.

At approximately 6 miles from the Pleasant Valley Trail, the road bends west and enters Berdoo Canyon. A turnout can be found here with a short hike following an old homesteader road, to the summit of a hill with a great view of Pleasant Valley and Geology Tour Road. The difficult "crux" section comes early on, just 1.5 miles further. Make it past the rocky wash and it's smooth sailing for almost the entire rest of the journey. There are many sections where the road splits and rejoins. Near the bottom of the canyon, intermittent sections of old and decaying asphalt road will be encountered which can actually be more difficult to negotiate than the wash. Eventually, the canyon will become huge berms of sand and cobblestones, runoff detritius from eons of erosion. This is where some interesting hill-climbing testpieces can be found. Upon exiting the mountain and canyon system, keep a sharp eye out for the exit road, which climbs a small berm on the right (W), gaining an asphalt road that travels south and joins with Dillion Road in Coachella Valley. Turn left on Dillion Road to reach Interstate 10 or, better yet, turn right and drive Dillion Road as it becomes a rollercoaster ride of small hills for the next 20 miles or so.

HIKE

Hexahedron Mine - #29

Total distance: 8.5 miles (round trip)
Physical difficulty: 4
Technical difficulty: 3
Navigating: 2
Trail type: mine road

The trek out to the Hexahedron Mine is the most difficult hike described in this book. Not only is it lengthy, but the second half is also quite strenuous, rising deep into the rugged Hexie Mountains. The highlight of this journey, aside from traversing some beautiful and remote desert terrain, is the Hexahedron stone house ruin. This roofless and slowly decaying ruin is a work of stone art with its colorful rock construction, two window openings, and a front entry. The house is fantastically located on a high ridge overlooking the entire Hexie Range, with vistas to Pleasant Valley, Pinto Basin, Stirrup Tank, and even the Pinto Wye area. Aside from the house, not much is left of the mining operation—a few shafts, adits, the usual trash heap, and an odd plowing device.

The late 1800s saw the first mining activity at the site, with Jep Ryan and his usual cohorts—Kelsey, Tingman, Holland, and the Garrison brothers—forming the Hexahedron Mining Company. The U.S. Bureau of Mines lists a sole record of gold production at the mine, 116 .68 ounces of placer gold, dated from 1893. Other information reports a 12-man crew working the site in the early 1900s, also citing a mill on or near the mine.

Top: Mine shaft at the Hexahedron, with the bunkhouse in the background.
Middle: Abandoned plowing device.
Bottom: Bat-friendly mine grating seals this shaft from curious humans.

The bunkhouse at the Hexahedron Mine, at sunset.

The hike starts out as a long, but easy, 3-mile stroll following an old mine road out across the flat ground of Pleasant Valley. Intermittent hard-packed dirt and sandy washes characterize the travel. Once at the far east end of Pleasant Valley, the old road ascends to a bench above the valley floor, where the road leading to the Hexahedron Mine begins its wicked-steep climb into the Hexie Mountains. The Hexie Mountains on this side are covered in shiny black rock and adorned with dwarf creosote bushes, bright red barrel cactus, and spikey hedgehog succulents. Four brutally steep switchbacks lead up the rocky hillside to a summit of sorts, where the road levels off for a bit. From there, the road gently rises, then decends, as it winds through the summit peaks to the mine site. The high vistas from the road as it treks across the top of the Hexies are simply awesome.

An interesting side trek can be taken that leads to a small stone house in a nearby wash. The Fried Liver Wash Stone House is a small and somewhat razed ruin consisting of four nearly completely crumbled stone walls with a toppled entryway. The dessicated remains of a wooden roof lie close by. The trek can be added to the Hexahedron Mine hike with less than 1 mile of additional distance, or the Fried Liver Wash Stone House can be done alone as a relatively easy 7-mile (round trip) walk across the flat ground of Pleasant Valley.

Details: Park at the Pleasant Valley Backcountry Board, located 12 miles south down Geology Tour Road. Follow the trail that heads east behind the board, leading over a small ridge in deep sand. Once over the ridge the trail becomes hard-packed

View of the White Tank Campground area on the trail to the Hexahedron Mine.

dirt, following an obvious mine road east through Pleasant Valley. Looking east through Pleasant Valley to the far horizon, one can see a small, rounded hill in the gap between the mountain ranges. This hill—which looks to be about 50 miles away, but it is really only 3 miles distant—is where the road leading into the Hexie Mountains, and ultimately to the Hexahedron Mine, is located. The first mile and a half across Pleasant Valley, is, for the lack of a better word, pleasant. The road is easy to follow, and the ground solid and nearly barren of all obstacles. The second mile and a half is also easy. In this section, the road crosses in and out of several paralleling washes, where there are some sections of thick sand. If you lose track of the road, no worries, just continue east toward the hill. Once at the hill, the road cuts an obvious path on the hill's left side, leading up to a bench above the wash. (Note: If going directly to the Fried Liver Wash Stone House, veer right around the hill and follow a huge wash as it veers back east behind the hill. The small stone structure is 1/2 mile down this wash.) From the bench, the visible scar of the road cuts diagonally right. Follow the road as it carves four brutal switchbacks to the summit of the first mountain. From there, the road levels off for a bit, then gently rises once again, cutting a sweeping curve around a second summit before descending slightly into the inner Hexie Mountains. Keep an eye out for the telltale tailings of the operation. The house will not come into view until you are right up on it. On the return trip down the mountain, it's possible to shortcut to the Fried Liver Wash Stone House: Once

The Pleasant Valley road/trail. The small hill in the gap marks the road/trail leading to the Hexahedron Mine.

down the mountain at the bench above Pleasant Valley, simply walk south, over the right shoulder of the hill, then veer left (E), eventually ending up in the huge wash. Look for the stone structure on the right (S) bank of the wash. Adding this side trek makes the whole hike 10 miles total distance.

Twilight at the stone house ruin in Fried Liver Wash.

A forest of Joshua trees, including the famous Barber Pole, dot the horizon in Queen Valley. Below: Lost Horse Valley figures.

THE JOSHUA TREE

Yucca brevifolia: The short-leafed yucca. Jedediah Smith called it the "Dirk Pear Tree" on his trek across the Mojave in 1827. To Spanish explorers it was izote de desierto, the Desert Dagger. Mormon pioneers likely coined it the "Joshua" tree, its arms raised in praise of the Lord. Early 1900s author J. Smeaton Chase writes: "It is a weird and menacing object, more like some conception of Poe or Doré than any work of wholesome mother nature ... A landscape filled with Joshua trees has a nightmare effect even in broad daylight; at the witching hour it can be almost infernal." Oh, what fantasies these strange figures conjure up, as if Hermann Rorschach himself fashioned them for some grand experiment of the imagination.

Not really a tree at all, this hearty member of the Lily family occupies a shallow ecological niche in the desert, only propagating at elevations between 2000 and 6000 feet, and only in deserts with higher-than-average precipitation. This iconic plant plays a central role in the ecology of the Mojave Desert. It has even been suggested that the Joshua tree's range is what delineates the Mojave Desert's

boundaries. It has also been suggested that this desert landmark is a sensitive indicator of climate change; some have warned that the Joshua tree may disappear from the Park altogether in the near future.

Odd growth patterns of the branches occur when the growing tip (the terminal bud) is damaged, causing the plant to branch off in random directions.

(continue on next page)

A Lost Horse giant basks in full-moon light on a warm summer evening.

(continued)

Damage typically occurs from boring insects, but the growth of a flower bud can also cause the limbs to branch off. Flowering occurs from February through April, when the Joshua tree produces a football-size cluster of creamy, greenish flowers. The tree propagates from both seeds and a long runner root that travels out from the parent tree, growing a line of offshoots along its path. Occasionally, a branch or even an entire tree can fall and survive, producing a cluster of

Roadside nightmare.   Inset: Detail of a Joshua tree bud.

tightly packed offshoots. Joshua trees are long-lived. Estimates vary, but the average Joshua tree is certainly several hundred years old, and some of the largest and oldest ones may be 500 years old or more. Tree-ring dating is, for the most part, impossible due to the pithy and fibrous trunk.

Early in the 1900s, the largest known Joshua tree was burned to create light for one evening. At the turn of this century, the largest known Joshua tree within Joshua Tree National Park boundaries fell. Located in the far western end of the Park, at Covington Flats, the behemoth was 45 feet tall! Dispite a general decline, healthy groves of Joshua trees blanket the entire Mojave portion of the Park. Lurking within the forests are some of the grandest, oldest, and strangest figures, standing in limbo, waiting to fuel our dreams ...

... and our nightmares!

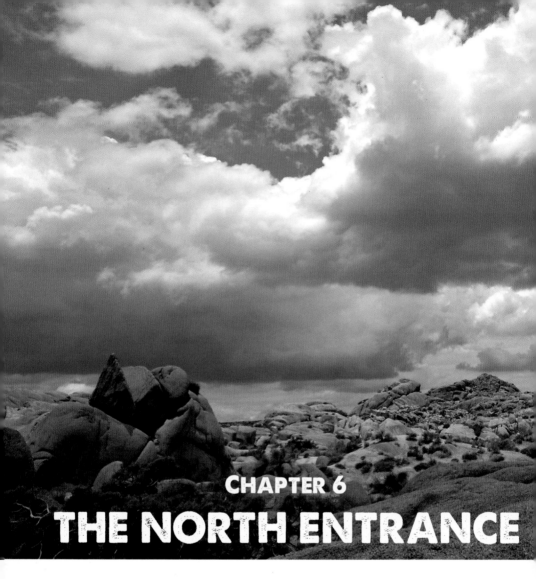

CHAPTER 6
THE NORTH ENTRANCE

The North Entrance is located just outside the town of 29 Palms. Utah Trail Road leads south into the Park, traveling gently uphill in a broad valley lined by rocky mountains. The visitors center can be found just after turning onto Utah Trail from Highway 62, in the town of 29 Palms. Along with the usual ameneties and information, the visitors center features a short trail leading out to the Oasis of Mara. The oasis was a prominent Native American village and one of the last known native dwellings in the area. Nothing remains of the village other than the spring and palm trees on which the inhabitants relied.

The Park entrance is another 3 miles south on Utah Trail, where the road changes name to Park Boulevard. About 1 mile before the entrance kiosk is a granite formation known as Joshua Mountain but often called the Indian Head, named because it vaguely resembles a Native American headdress. A short but brutal hike leads up the gully below the formation, ending at the base of the rock. A flat area at the summit offers a bit of exploring.

The famous Dwarf Juniper (see page 175) weathering another storm, while Jumbo Rocks Campground hides in the rocks below.

Once inside the Park, several hikes can be found leading to various mines, including the Contact Mine. After approximately 4 miles, the road begins to weave through some hills, then makes a broad curve to the west to a junction, referred to as the Pinto Wye. The intersecting road is Pinto Basin Road, which leads south past a few small campgrounds and then eastward as it heads down into Pinto Basin, eventually making its way to the East Entrance and Interstate 10 about 40 miles distant.

Past the Pinto Wye, Park Boulevard forges west as it continues to climb into the high plateau of central Joshua Tree. Signature granite rock piles will begin to come into view, with several short turnoffs leading to rocky formations. Here you will find Live Oak Picnic Area and Split Rock. Both areas offer walks, sights, and lots of rocks to crawl around on and explore. Approximately 1 mile west of the Split Rock/Live Oak intersection on Park Boulevard is a geological curiosity named Skull Rock, identified by a crosswalk in the road and, typically, hordes of people. (Slow down here, as the chances of a pedestrian aimlessly wandering into the road are high!) Park at paved pullouts at the crosswalk and walk 20 yards to view the rock close up. Just past Skull Rock on Park Boulevard is Jumbo Rocks Campground, quite possibly the best campground in Joshua Tree.

   Back at the Pinto Wye, a south turn takes you onto Pinto Basin Road. The road will first pass two small and pleasant campgrounds, Belle and White Tank. The latter hosts one of the more popular sights in the Park, Arch Rock. A short and well-marked trail leads from the campground to the arch. Several artificial catchments can also be seen further along on the trail. Just past White Tank Campground on Pinto Basin Road is a dirt road heading off southwest; this leads to Stirrup Tank. Not much to see here, but there are some scattered rock piles that can fun to wander through. A small rock pile at the junction has some interesting graffiti from the late 1800s. Continuing south, Pinto Basin Road enters a canyon that weaves through hills on its way down into Pinto Basin (see Chapter 7).

The Indian Head, located a mile north of the North Entrance. The rugged approach travels up the gully in the center of the photo.

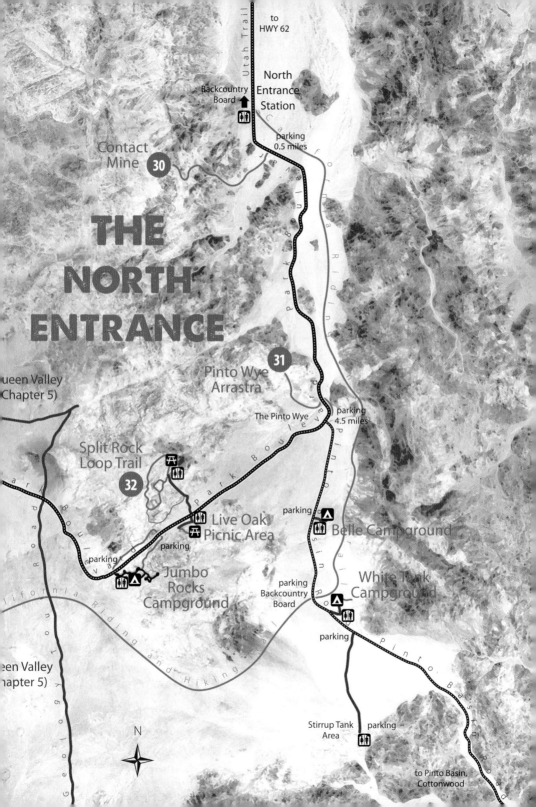

to HWY 62

Utah Trail

Backcountry
Board

North
Entrance
Station

parking
0.5 miles

California Riding and Hiking Trail

Contact
Mine **30**

THE
NORTH
ENTRANCE

Queen Valley
(Chapter 5)

Park Boulevard

Pinto Wye
Arrastra **31**

The Pinto Wye

parking
4.5 miles

Split Rock
Loop Trail **32**

Park Boulevard

Live Oak
Picnic Area

parking

parking

Jumbo
Rocks
Campground

Pinto Basin Road

parking

Belle Campground

White Tank
Campground

parking
Backcountry
Board

parking

California Riding and Hiking Trail

Geology Tour Road

Queen Valley
(Chapter 5)

Stirrup Tank
Area

parking

to Pinto Basin,
Cottonwood

N

HIKE
Contact Mine - #30

Total distance: 3.5 miles (round trip)
Physical difficulty: 3
Technical difficulty: 2
Navigating: 2
Trail type: official/mine road

**The Contact Mine Trail is an excellent
hike into the rugged hills near the
North Entrance. The trail is well marked,
heading up a very large drainage before
following the old mine road that leads to
the mine site. The road winds deep into
the rugged mountains, traversing slopes of
dark rock and meandering across rolling hills
sprinkled with bright red barrel cactus.**

   **The early 1900s operation was
moderately successful, unearthing a fair
amount of both gold and silver. The site
has several pieces of machinery remaining;
several cable winches, an engine and
piston pump, and typical scattered debris.**

Top: Mine cart track leading from the mine out to the edge of the hill, which has been eroded away. Middle: Cable winch and other machinery remaining at the site. Bottom: The Park Service has recently upgraded this trail, making it easy to follow.

Left Top: The old road, with the mine site in the distance.
Left Bottom: Barrel cactus proliferate on the slopes leading
out to the mine. Above: Old motor, with mine grate behind.

**Also remaining are sections of mining
cart track. The road/trail leading up to
the mine, cut into the rugged hillside, is
impressive in itself, a testament to the
stubborn tenacity of the miners.**

Details: Park at the large turnout and
information board located on the west side
of the road 0.5 miles from the North Entrance
station. A well-marked trail leads to the west.
The trail will turn into a wash, which becomes
large and sandy. This section is marked with
obvious red signage. After 0.5 miles, the main
wash will bend to the right, passing near the
rocky hillside. Either continue in the wash or
stay on the marked trail (a bit easier to walk
on) as it ascends a small embankment on the
left, paralleling the wash on its way into the
hills. A bit futher on, the trail crosses the wash
and begins to ascend the hillside. The road
is obvious from here. Follow it as it bends
right, then arcs around to the left, ascending
relentlessly for the next 0.25 miles. Eventually
the road levels off, then bends to the right
again, heading into an upper canyon. The
road will continue to bend to the right until it's
traveling north. The telltale pilings of the mine
will come into view on the distant hillside near
the top of the canyon. The final 50 yards of the
journey are particularly rugged; time has not
been kind to the road.

HIKE

Pinto Wye Arrastra - #31

Total distance: 1 mile (round trip)
Physical difficulty: 2
Technical difficulty: 1
Navagating: 2
Trail type: cross-country

This beautiful piece of early 1900s mining machinery is tucked away in a quiet canyon, isolated from the hustle and bustle of Park Boulevard, located just a couple hundred yards distant. A range of hills separating the location from the road gives it that remote feel. The relatively easy hike travels cross-country (read: no trail!), passing though a sandy wash lined with interestingly shaped rocks, then up onto an open plateau. The route then drops down into the secluded wash that leads to the site. The hills are dotted with barrel cactus and occasional mines. (Danger: Some of the mines in this area are unsealed and should not be entered.)

**   Not much to see at the site, with the exception of the small arrasta, an ore grinder similar to a mill. Large stones are attached to a central post, where they rotate around inside a circular trough, grinding small rocks into fine powder. A placard below the arrasta describes what it is and how it works, as well as its status on the National Register of Historical Places. This arrasta is well preserved and is a fine example of early 1900s mining technology.**

Details: There are two possible ways to reach the site. Other guides suggest parking roadside on Park Boulevard 0.5 miles north of the "Pinto Wye" junction with Pinto Basin Road, then hiking west over the hill, following a prominent drainage. A second approach, albeit a bit longer, is recommended here. Park at a turnout on Park Boulevard 100

Top: The unique and excellently preserved arrastra.
Middle: Chockstone in the nearby wash.

yards northeast of the Pinto Wye. Walk north along Park Boulevard for several hundred yards past a small wash to a very large wash that crosses the road. Turn left (W) and head up the wash, which becomes a small canyon lined with rocks. When the small canyon opens up to a broad wash, veer to the right (NW) and walk up the hillside to a flat plain. From there, travel north behind the range of hills that parallels Park Boulevard. Drop down into a wash that leads north and continue down it for maybe 400 yards. Keep an eye out for the arrasta on the right side of the wash, slightly up on the hillside with a small placard in front of it. There are several mines above it.

The dwarf juniper and monolith, shot under the stars with rising moonlight.

Looking west from the Split Rock parking loop. Aside from the listed hikes, the area has many corridors to explore and tabletop domes to ascend.

SPLIT ROCK

Split Rock is named after the obvious broken boulder at the north end of the parking loop. Behind and below the boulder is a large cave. The end parking lot contains several picnic tables and restrooms. Many climber trails, and one official trail, head off in all directions from the parking lot. Any of these trails will make for a pleasant walk, and the many corridors and canyons just beg for exploration.

The Split Rock Loop Trail is the headliner here. It's a relatively mild 2.5-mile stroll along gently rolling desert terrain, through sandy washes, and across rocky terraces. The trail passes through many unusually shaped rock formations, some of which have garnered interesting names: Tulip Rock, Orangutan Rock, and the Brain. The path is well marked and easy to follow.

For those looking for a bit of adventure, check out the so-called Cling or Fling Corridor. This chasm, christened by rock climbers, makes for a tidy adventure, located just minutes from the car. Entering the chasm requires a bit of hands-on rock scrambling.

Split Rock is located off of Park Boulevard, 2.2 miles west of the "Pinto Wye" (6.7 miles from the North Entrance), or 10 miles east of Intersection Rock (19 miles from West Entrance). Look for the 4-way intersection on Park Boulevard and turn north (south leads to Live Oak Picnic Area) and take this dirt road for approximately 1 mile to its end.

Right: Split Rock. Yarns have been spun as to the origin of the fracture, some even involving aliens. Splits like this are in fact quite common in this type of rock.

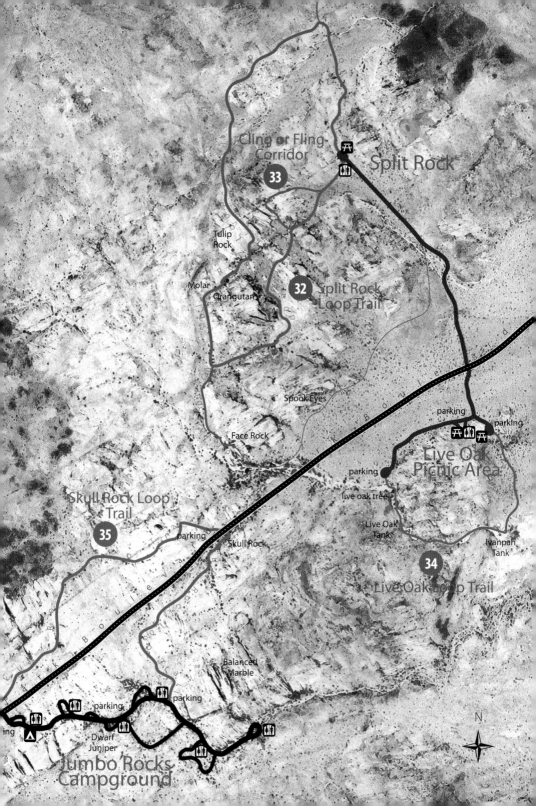

Cling or Fling
Corridor

33

Split Rock

Tulip
Rock

Molar

Orangutan

32

Split Rock
Loop Trail

Spook Eyes

Face Rock

parking

parking

Live Oak
Picnic Area

parking

live oak tree

Skull Rock Loop
Trail

Live Oak
Tank

35

parking

Ivanpah
Tank

Skull Rock

34

Live Oak Loop Trail

Balanced
Marble

parking

parking

Dwarf
Juniper

Jumbo Rocks
Campground

ing

N

HIKE

Split Rock Loop Trail - #32

Total distance: 2-mile loop
Physical difficulty: 2
Technical difficulty: 1
Navagating: 1
Trail type: official trail

The Split Rock Loop Trail is a lesser-known gem in the Joshua Tree trail system. The well-marked trail travels through classic Joshua Tree terrain, across rolling plains of juniper and Spanish dagger, through deep sandy washes, beneath towering granite rock piles, and among fantastically sculpted boulders. Many of the rocks here assume unusual shapes, prompting visitors to let their imaginations go wild. Tulip Rock is a formation that has a tulip-shaped bulb sitting on its summit. Ghost and Goblin Rocks greet you along the trail. If you keep a sharp eye out, you may see Orangutan Rock peering at you from his high perch. Still other rocks resemble human faces, and there's even a large brain baking in the hot desert air! Balanced rocks, marbles, egg clutches, and even a few arches can be found along the path. A short spur trail leads off to Face Rock. In addition to its profile visage, at least three other faces can be seen here, including an elven dwarf and Jimmy Durante.

Details: It's possible to walk this trail in either direction but it is described here in a counterclockwise direction. From the end parking loop, follow the trail that leaves its north side. (The trailhead can be found just left of the namesake Split Rock.) Continue around to the back of the large boulder, where a large cave is located. On a warm day this cave is a great place to beat the heat! Follow

Top: Tulip Rock
Middle: Orangutan Rock
Bottom: Old cattle trough near Face Rock

the trail north as it weaves over and around boulders before dropping down into a sandy wash. The trail continues north, across rolling terrain and crossing several more washes before rising onto a hillside and turning to the left (W). The trail continues west for a little over 1/2 mile, passing many rock piles enroute. Eventually the trail will bend left (SW), heading back into the rockpiles. Keep an eye out for the aforementioned rock shapes in this area! Continue on, weaving through a pass between large boulders and then to a flat area, where the trail enters a wash. Look for a sign in the wash noting a junction in the trail: Left leads back to the parking lot, right is a short spur trail leading to Face Rock. Once at Face Rock, backtrack the trail to return.

Top: Spook eyes and a balanced rock, seen along the unofficial continuation of the Face Rock spur trail. Bottom: Face Rock, sometimes said to resemble George Washington.

Alternately, if you don't mind a bit of cross-county travel, continue from Face Rock through a constriction in the wash and turn left (E), following a sandy wash that parallels Park Boulevard. When the wash bends toward the road, exit left and continue east until the Split Rock entrance road is encountered. Turn left and follow the dirt road back to the parking lot (2.5 miles for this off-trail variation).

HIKE

Cling or Fling Corridor - #33

Total distance: 0.75 miles (round trip)
Physical difficulty: 2
Technical difficulty: 3
Navagating: 2
Trail type: cross-country/rock scrambling

This is another gem, known mostly only to the rock-climbing community. The rock formation is actually cleaved by two corridors, or crevices, but one is choked with brush (I have been through; it's not that fun!). This is a good hike to do on a hot day, as the corridors are usually cool and shady.

The trail starts across an open ridge, then quickly enters a pleasant alcove of rock. Interesting quartz dikes streak the rolling granite floor of the alcove. At the back of the alcove, a bit of boulder hopping leads to both corridors. The Cling or Fling Corridor, the thinner and more dramatic of the two, is 10 feet wide, 75 feet long, and has a huge stone lodged near the top. It requires a bit of climbing down boulders to get into, and also a bit of climbing to get out of! Once on the other side, a rugged gully leads down into the open flats and joins with the final leg of the Split Rock Loop Trail.

Details: From the end parking loop, head west on the well-trodden trail (the end of the Split Rock Loop Trail). After about 50 yards, veer to the right and walk toward the rock pile, continuing northwest for another 100 yards. Look for a large boulder. An alcove lies behind (W of) the boulder. Scramble over boulders to reach the back of the alcove, where there are two corridors. The corridor on the left leads to the south and is worth checking out; it's a more open corridor with a sandy base, and usually, a nice breeze. Back in the right (NW) side of the alcove is

Top: The hidden entrance to the corridor.
Middle: Looking through Cling or Fling Corridor.

the Cling or Fling Corridor. Drop down into the crevice. The corridor's floor is somewhat choked with boulders, so be prepared for a bumpy ride. Once through and on the other side, head left (S) down the gully, following a faint trail down onto flat ground that rejoins the Split Rock Loop Trail. Turn left here, heading east, back to the parking loop.

LIVE OAK PICNIC AREA

The Live Oak Picnic Area is a small group of rock formations with parking, restrooms, and day-use picnic sites strewn around the base. The area gets its name from the very large and rare Live Oak tree growing in a wash at the area's west end. The easily accessed rocks here hide many corridors and nooks that are great for exploring, and the highly eroded nature of the granite makes for a scenic backdrop. For those looking to get out and about, there are several interesting tanks (dams) that can be found in a wash behind the rock formations. One of the tanks, called Ivanpah Tank, is quite large by Joshua Tree standards, and has been known to accumulate a small lake behind it in wetter seasons.

The Live Oak Picnic Area is located across from the turnoff to Split Rock on Park Boulevard, 2.2 miles west of the Pinto Wye (6.7 miles from the North Entrance), or 10 miles east of Intersection Rock (19 miles from West Entrance). Turn south at the junction and follow a dirt road for several hundred yards to the area. Head straight in and park for direct access to the tanks. Turn right and park at the end loop for the Live Oak Loop Trail.

The unusual live oak growing in the wash at Live Oak picnic area.

The downstream side of Ivanpah Tank. The upstream side has filled with sediment to within five feet of the top of the dam.

HIKE

Live Oak Loop Trail - #34

Total distance: 0.9-mile loop
Physical difficulty: 2
Technical difficulty: 1
Navagating: 1
Trail type: wash travel/old road

The Live Oak Loop Trail encircles the entire group of rock formations at the Live Oak Picnic Area. The trail starts in a deep, sandy wash passing the majestic Live Oak tree, most likely planted by cattle ranchers in the early 1900s. Granite spires and boulders tower overhead in this section of the wash. The largest of these spires is aptly named the Pope's Hat. Further down the wash, the trail passes by a small stone wall that creates Live Oak Tank. The sands of time (heh) have filled this tank almost completely. It's easy to overlook, so keep a sharp eye out for it in the wash. As the wash bends to the east it begins to broaden, becoming the small basin behind the impressive Ivanpah Tank. If you're very lucky, this basin will have a

beautiful small lake captured behind it, but it's usually just a grassy depression. Continue around to the east side of the dam to truly appreciate its stature. The final leg of the journey follows an old dirt road.

Details: You can reach Ivanpah Tank directly by parking on the east side of the picnic area and walking an old dirt road that heads south. After 500 yards, the road ends above a wash, with Ivanpah Tank directly below. For the Live Oak Loop Trail, park on the west side of the picnic area. From the small parking loop, head south, immediately dropping down into a large, sandy wash and walking to the obvious live oak tree. Live Oak Tank is approximately 150 yards down the wash. Continue down the rocky wash as it gradually bends to the east (hiker's left). It is 0.4 miles to Ivanpah Tank from the parking loop. Once at Ivanpah Tank, ascend the left bank of the wash and follow an old dirt road north to reach the parking area. From there, walk the road, turning left to reach the starting point.

SKULL ROCK

Skull Rock is but one of the many strangly eroded rocks to be found in this general area; this one vaguely resembles a human skull. It has also been referred to as "The Bogieman," as it kinda lurkes behind the bushes alongside the road. Skull Rock can be found midway between the Split Rock/Live Oak junction and Jumbo Rocks Campground. A large turnout area and a painted crosswalk mark the starting point, and the rock is located a mere 25 yards from the turnouts.

JUMBO ROCK CAMPGROUND

Jumbo Rocks Campground is quite possibly the best campground in Joshua Tree National Park. It is quite a large campground, with sites nestled inside a maze of rocky alcoves and cul-de-sacs. Many sites have a secluded feel despite the many others all around. The low-lying "tabletop" domes that create the rock maze offer lots of opportunities for wandering, and the campground's location on the cusp of the open desert becons the adventurous to explore.

Some of the most interesting rock formations in the Park can be found here. Time and the elements have transformed the loose, easily eroded granite into fantastic shapes and configurations. Many of Joshua Tree's most iconic landscapes are located in and around Jumbo Rocks Campground. The exquisite Monolith and Dwarf Juniper are highly prized by photographers (it's worth mentioning that some years ago, a witless camper illegally sawed off one of the branches of this little treasure to make a campfire), not to mention the Balancing Marble and Jagged Spires. Skull Rock is just a short walk away, and the Split Rock Loop Trail can be accessed across the street from the campground's entrance.

The Balancing Marble, with a second marble mimicking the first.

Jumbo Rocks Campground is located off of Park Boulevard, approximately 8 miles southwest from the North Entrance (3.6 miles west of the Pinto Wye), or 19 miles east of the West Entrance (10 miles east of Intersection Rock). A fee kiosk and restrooms can be found near the entrance to the campground (see introduction for camping information). For those visiting the area but not camping, parking can be found either along Park Boulevard at the campground entrance, or just after turning into the campground. There are several small day-use parking areas further in the campground (at 0.2 miles and 0.4 miles). Be warned that driving in the campground can be confusing with all of the spur loops!

HIKE

Skull Rock Loop Trail - #35

Total distance: 1.7-mile loop
Physical difficulty: 2
Technical difficulty: 1
Navagating: 1
Trail type: official trail

Skull Rock as seen from the road. The rock has also been nicknamed the Bogieman, as many drivers passing by in the night have been spooked by the ominous figure lurking in the bushes.

There are three possible starting points: the turnout at Skull Rock, turnouts at the entrance to Jumbo Rocks Campground, and inside the campground (0.4 miles from entrance). The latter is the official starting point, and a small board displays details of the trail. From the campground trailhead, the trail meanders along the tops of low-lying granite domes on its way to Skull Rock 0.5 miles away. Beautifully sculpted granite crags and boulders can be viewed along this stretch. From Skull Rock, the trail crosses the road and heads north for 100 yards or so before taking a sharp left and traveling west into more beautifully sculpted beds of rock. In this area, the domes form many thin corridors that beg to be explored. After another 0.75 miles the trail will once again cross the road (S). The final leg of the trail travels down the main campground road to the starting point.

Details: This description is from the trailhead inside the campground, 0.4 miles from the entrance. Park at the Amphitheater turnout and locate the trailhead on the opposite side of the road. Take the trail northeast to Skull Rock 0.5 miles distant. From there, cross the road and follow the obvious trail uphill (N). At the top of the hill the trail will turn left (W), passing through a corridor and dropping into a large, sandy wash. Follow the wash for several hundred yards until it ends, continuing on the trail southwest. The trail will parallel the road for a bit before ending at a crosswalk. Cross the road and walk into the campground, following the main road back to the starting point.

Perhaps the most sought-after photo-op in the Park: the Dwarf Juniper and Monolith, here shot during a stormy sunset.

Photography notes:

Jumbo Rocks Campground and the area surrounding it is a treasure trove for photographers. Eroded rocks of all shapes and sizes can be found teetering and juxtaposed, strewn across the tabletop domes that cover the area. Aside from the endless compositional possibilities, the area contains two of the most sought-after photographic locations in the Park: The sublime Monolith and Dwarf Juniper, and the intriguing Balancing Marble and Jagged Spire. These locations are just a stone's throw away from each other.

Monolith and Dwarf Juniper: Park at the day-use parking 0.2 miles inside the campground, then walk east for 50 yards and turn right (S) into the campground loop. Look straight ahead for the small tree at the top of a hill, another 60 yards distant. Scramble up the hillside to the left of the tree (please do not walk through occupied campsites). The tree gets nice light in both the morning and afternoon, and is also a favorite for night photos.

Balancing Marble and Jagged Spires: Park at the day-use "Amphitheater" parking 0.4 miles inside the campground. Locate the Skull Rock trailhead across the road (slightly east). Take the trail eastward as it travels uphill. After about 100 yards, veer to the right and walk onto the top of the low-lying tabletop dome. The cliff should be obvious by now, another 100 yards to the east. This location is best shot in the late afternoon.

Another highly desired photographic location: Arch Rock. The arch is prized by night photographers as it sits elevated above the surrounding rocks. Photographed here under a full moon.

PINTO BASIN ROAD

Pinto Basin Road intersects Park Boulevard at the Pinto Wye. Heading south, the road travels over a gently domed plain, passing several pleasant campgrounds on its way down into Pinto Basin. The highlight of this area is the beautiful Arch Rock. The arch is one of those "must-have" souvenir photo locations. A short trail leads through White Tank Campground and on to the arch, where highly sculpted granite rocks and several tanks (small damsites) can also be seen. Further down Pinto Basin Road, a dirt road on the right leads southwest to the Stirrup Tank rock piles. At the junction is a parking lot, where nearby, graffitti from the late 1800s can be seen on a large boulder. Nothing too remarkable to see at Stirrup Tank, but it is a nice place to wander between the many rocks and deep, sandy washes. Beyond the turnoff to Stirrup Tank, Pinto Basin Road crests a pass at Wilson Canyon, dropping down into Pinto Basin.

BELLE CAMPGROUND

Belle is a pleasant little campground sitting out on the open plains of Joshua Tree, situated near a large and somewhat lonely dome of granite. The campground is small and highly desirable, so the chances of getting a site in peak season are slim. Unfortunately, the campground is also closed in summer. Those who do get a site may be treated to the "alien" light shows that are often seen to the north. It's possible that these shows may be caused by night war games taking place on at the 29 Palms Marine Base, north of the town of 29 Palms.

WHITE TANK CAMPGROUND

White Tank is a beautiful campground nestled among outcroppings of highly sculpted granite. As with Belle, it is a small and highly desirable campground; finding a vacant site can be hit-or-miss. The campground sits on the edge of a large granite boulderfield, offering lots of nearby exploring. The wonderful Arch Rock trail starts from the north end of the campground. Visitor parking, as well as an information board and campground fee kiosk, are found near the entrance of the campground.

Highly fractured and easily eroded, the rock around White Tank Campground assumes many strange forms.

CHAPTER 7
PINTO BASIN

Pinto Basin encompasses just about the entire eastern half of Joshua Tree National Park. At roughly 6 miles wide and 30 miles long, it is the largest valley in the Park. This side of Joshua Tree lies in the Colorado Desert zone, a sub-classification of the larger Sonoran Desert. Creosote and jumping cholla dominate the landscape. One of the more noticable differences in this section of the Park is the lack of Joshua trees, which only grow in the higher elevations of the Park. Another difference is the distinct absence of granite cliffs and rock formations. Indeed, Pinto Basin seems like a giant bowl of nothing! In fact, nothing could not be further from the truth. Pinto Basin has many interesting sights and activities that are unique to the Park.

The most popular attraction in this section of Joshua Tree is the Cholla Cactus Garden. Growing high on the western tip of Pinto Basin is this humongous patch of Teddy Bear Cholla. A short and "painless" trail meanders through the patch, fenced off to protect the chollas from the vicious feet of visitors—ha! About a mile east of that is an ocotillo patch. Not quite as impressive as the cholla patch, the ocotillo patch has around 50 plants, some of which are quite large.

The entire rim of Pinto Basin is lined with mines and mining camps. This book lists several of the more interesting ones, but there are many many more to be explored, some well documented, others completely off the radar.

Ore bins at the Silver Bell Mine sit high on a ridge overlooking the western end of Pinto Basin.

If you are into four-wheeling, there are a couple of old mining roads that cut across Pinto Basin and into the rugged hills surrounding the basin, either of which will make for a good day of 4x4-ing. Both roads travel through old mining districts in the Park, passing many mining sites and ruins along the way. Old Dale Road travels a steep, rocky, rutted road leading north out of the Park. Black Eagle Rock Mine Road cuts through deep washes and across rolling hills before heading through a mountain pass to the massive Black Eagle Rock Mine.

Pinto Basin was also home to ancient native peoples. The oldest known culture in this region lived along what is thought to be an ancient river that coursed through Pinto Basin near the end of the last ice age. "Pinto Man" sites have been discovered along this extinct river course, with artifacts dating back 4000 to 8000 years. This ancient culture's artifacts bear little resemblance to more modern native cultures (Serrano, Cahuilla, Chemihuevi), suggesting that Pinto culture disappeared from this region many thousands of years ago.

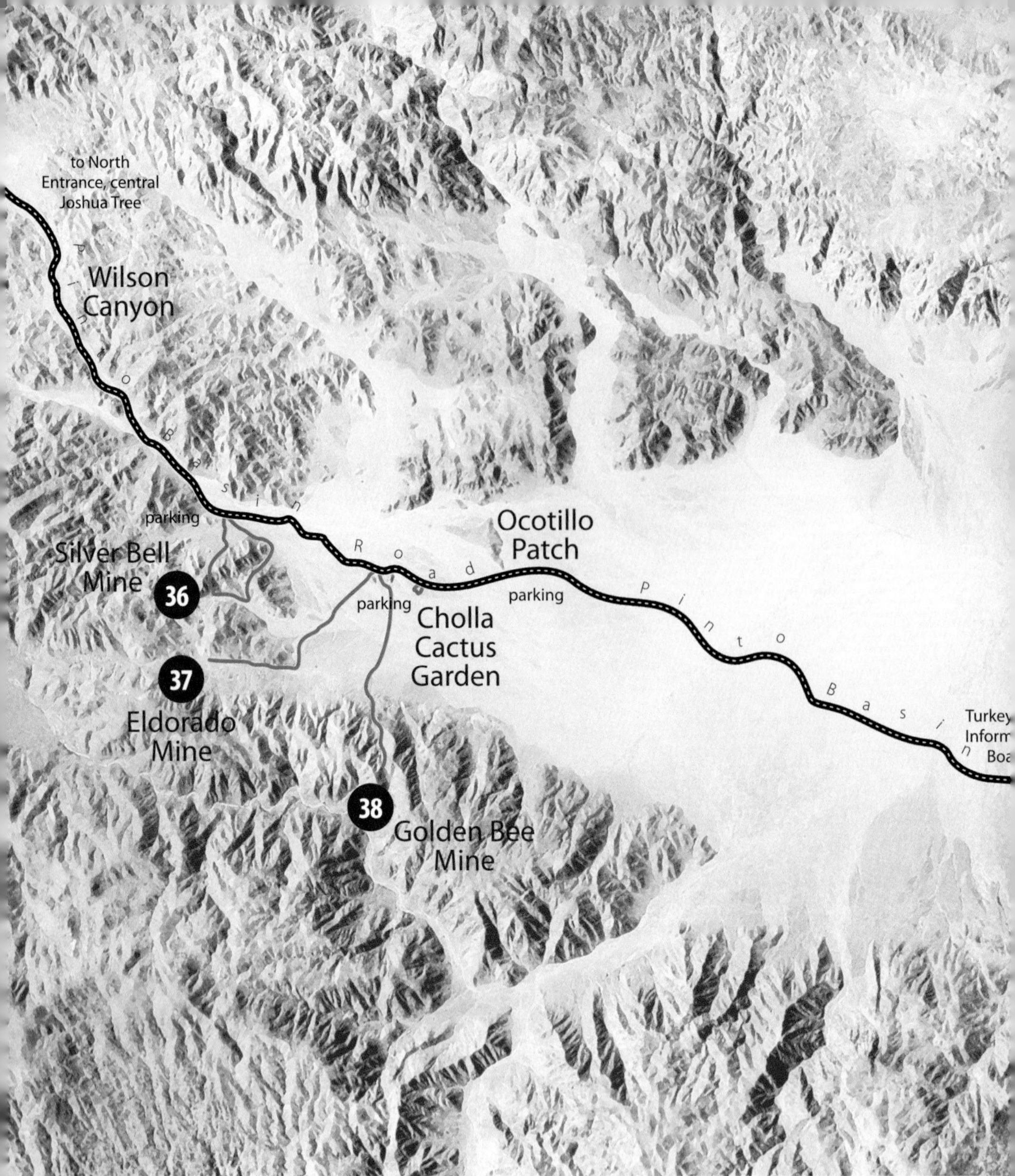

to North
Entrance, central
Joshua Tree

Wilson
Canyon

Pinto Basin Road

parking

Silver Bell
Mine

36

Ocotillo
Patch

parking

parking

Cholla
Cactus
Garden

37

Eldorado
Mine

Pinto Basin

Turkey
Inform
Boa

38

Golden Bee
Mine

WILSON CANYON

Traveling south on Pinto Basin Road past the turnoff to Stirrup Tank, you will enter a deep canyon alongside a sandy wash. Smoke trees dot the wash in this picturesque canyon. As the road winds its way through the canyon, it begins to descend more steeply, dropping down toward Pinto Basin. Several old mines can be seen on the hillsides near the bottom of the canyon. Once the canyon opens up, the vastness of Pinto Basin is revealed, with the view to the opposite side stretching to the horizon. Several small turnouts can be found here allowing visitors to stop and take it all in.

to HWY 62

Old Dale Road

Mission Well
Mill Site

Mission Well

Old Dale Road

N

PINTO
BASIN

Pinto Basin

Old Dale Road

Black Eagle Mine Road

Porcupine Wash
Backcountry
Board

Old Dale Road

Old Dale/Black Eagle
Information Board

to Cottonwood,
South Entrance

WEST SIDE OF PINTO BASIN

Pinto Basin is a very long, east-west trending valley. Its west side slopes gently downhill toward the middle of the basin, and both the north and south sides are lined with steep, rugged mountains. Three excellent mine sites can be found here: the Silver Bell, The Eldorado, and the Golden Bee, collectively known as the Hexie Mine Group. All three sites are littered with interesting mining relics, structures, and equipment.

Visitors traveling from the west will encounter the Hexie Mine Group shortly after Wilson Canyon. Two large wooden ore bins at the Silver Bell Mine can be seen on the closest hillside just south of the road. The Golden Bee Mine is a little more difficult to see, located near the top of a deep canyon on the mountainside across the valley to the south. The large wash leading to the Eldorado Mine is also visible across the valley to the south. As Pinto Basin Road continues to descend eastward into Pinto Basin, it passes near two small volcanic hills. These hills mark the launching point for the Eldorado and Golden Bee mines. Just east of the hills is the Cholla Cactus Garden.

HIKE

Silver Bell Mine - #36

Total distance: 2.2-mile loop
Physical difficulty: 3
Technical difficulty: 2
Navigating: 2
Trail type: cross-country/mine road

The Silver Bell Mine is the westernmost of the three mines in the Hexie Mine Group. It is located high on a hillside just south of the road, identified by two large wooden ore bins overlooking the whole of Pinto Basin. A turnout can be found on Pinto Basin Road below the mine, with an information board giving interesting facts about the operation. There is no official trail here as of yet, but a small path has formed behind the board, leading to the base of the mountain where an obvious road cuts into the hillside and travels straight up to the site. The views from the ore bins' high perch are spectacular. The path continues on behind this initial area, and the scope of the operation is revealed. Terraced digs and adits spill all the way down the back of the mountain to the canyon wash below. Hikers have the option of descending this treacherous hillside to the base of the site, or walking a faint trail diagonally down the back of the mountain to a second operation, known as the Golden Bell Mine (not to be confused with the nearby

Top: Ore bins high on the ridge; also visible is the steep road leading to the mine. Middle: Separating tub embedded in sludge.

Golden Bee Mine). Visiting the Golden Bell is discouraged by the Park Service because of dangerous unsealed vertical mine shafts in its vicinity. Give wide berth to these shafts as you investigate the interesting mining machinery and other relics from the bygone era. From the Golden Bell Mine, another weather-ravaged old road leads north down

the canyon and back toward Pinto Basin Road. At the mouth of this canyon are the faint remains of a shanty camp, where the tidy outlines for rows of tents can be seen on the ground.

Details: At the mouth of Wilson Canyon, on the south side of Pinto Basin Road, find a paved turnout with an information board about the Silver Bell Mine. Park here. The wooden ore bins and road cut leading to them should easily be visible. Follow a small trail behind the board, which soon dissipates into open desert, for 0.3 miles to where the roadcut meets the desert floor. Take the steep and rutted road to the wooden ore bins. Continue on the road to the flat mined area behind the hill. From this location there are options: Either walk a faint trail across the hillside to go directly to the Golden Bell Mine (watch for dangerous unsealed vertical shafts on this path), or for the complete loop, walk down the dangerously steep and rocky hillside to the lower part of the Silver Bell operation. Once at the valley floor, walk east in the wash for 100 yards or so, looking out for the road leading north (to the left)

Above: Old ore chute at the Golden Bee Mine.
Below: Desert gold in its many forms.

back up a side canyon and hill to the Golden Bell Mine. Watch for dangerous unsealed shafts in this area, too. From the saddle of the hill, continue north down the canyon on the almost non-existent road back to flat ground. Back on the desert floor, veer left and wrap around the toe of the mountain, following one of several small washes that lead north across the open desert. Keep a sharp eye out for the parking turnout on the right, which is not visible until you are right up on it.

HIKE
Eldorado Mine - #37

Total distance: 3 miles (round trip)
Physical difficulty: 2
Technical difficulty: 1
Navigating: 3
Trail type: cross-country/wash

Many of the hiking guides that cover Eldorado Mine describe a trek starting from Pleasant Valley, along the Geology Tour Road, and hiking 8.5 miles through a canyon to the mine, then continuing east to a shuttle car left on Pinto Basin Road. True, this is a beautiful hike, albeit quite long and somewhat inconvenient (arranging a return ride and all), but it is possible to just hike directly 1.5 miles to the mine from Pinto Basin Road, as described here.

This direct route travels across an ancient alluvial fan that is bisected by several large washes. Creosote, hedgehog cactus, cholla, and ocotillo decorate the landscape. A faint and intermittent mine road makes for easier footing in the second half of the journey, traveling at a modest

Top: Collapsed wooden structure overlooking the mine site. Middle: This 50-gallon drum, embedded in 100 years of wash sediment, makes a nice planter for Mother Nature.

grade up to a very large wash spilling out of a canyon in the mountain range. The final leg of the hike travels up this steep wash, traversing rocky banks and deep sand, as it heads into the canyon. The canyon walls are composed of exotic dark rock. Red barrel cactus clings tenaciously to the steep ramparts, standing out vibrantly against the near-black stone. Mining debris becomes more frequent in the wash close to the mine site.

The mine is about a third of the way up the canyon. A tailings pile high on the hillside comes into view first, then a small mountain of pinkish slag in the middle of the wash. At the site are several collapsed wood structures with the usual tin-can heap behind. In the wash is an unusual structure made of steel plates and concrete, possibly used in the processing of the crushed ore. The mine shafts are high on the steep hillside. It's possible to grind straight up the side of the hill to reach them, but a better option is to walk 100 yards up the wash, then back on a mine road cut into the hillside. Up at the mine, more interesting debris can be found, including round metal ore containers, wooden constructions, and concrete machinery foundations. The shafts here are sealed.

The Eldorado Mine was reportedly in production from the start of the 1900s to the 1940s. It was unique in that it produced a wider variety of metals and ores than other mines within the Park, including vanadium, galena, molybdenite, wulfenite, and, of course, gold.

Above: Diggings, slag, and cyanide tanks.
Below: Old cans and buckets.

Details: Park next to the two small volcanic hills on the south side of Pinto Basin Road, located 1/3 mile west of the Cholla Cactus Garden. This is more or less the closest point to the mine, and the hills make good reference points to find your vehicle on the return.) Head cross-country SSW toward the corner of the valley. There, a large wash spills out of a canyon, traveling along the base of the southern mountain front. The mine is located west up the wash, about a third of the way through the canyon. A very faint old mine road runs along the hills to the west, leading to the start of the target wash and the Eldorado Mine, but it is quite difficult to spot. The wash and entrance to the canyon are approximately 1.25 miles from the road. At the wash, turn left (W) and trudge uphill into the canyon, forging over rocky embankments and through deep sand. The mine is another 0.25 miles up the canyon. Look for the telltale tailings pile on the rightside (N) hillside. The rest of the operation is in the wash below.

Left: An unusual "floating" structure sitting alongside an impressive mound of slag.

Nighttime at the Ocotillo Patch, Pinto Basin Road.

HIKE

Golden Bee Mine - #38

Total distance: 4 miles (round trip)
Physical difficulty: 3
Technical difficulty: 3
Navigating: 3
Trail type: cross-country/mine road

Top: Ore bin with a wheelbarrow plank and a grand view.
Middle: Collapsed structures and furniture at basecamp.

This adventure follows an old mine road out across the vast Pinto Basin and up into the rugged Hexie Mountains to the south. The first 1.5 miles is easy traveling across a flat desert of creosote, cholla, and other pricklies. The final 0.5 miles up the canyon is brutally steep, with that final wooden ore bin sitting at the very top of the canyon, egging hikers on like a carrot on a stick!

    The old road/trail starts out across hard-packed desert, slightly decending on its way across the basin. Further along, a stand of large chollas can be seen a few hundred yards to the west of the road, a pristine version of the Cholla Cactus Garden. Running along the base of the mountain is a very large, rocky, and complex wash, which is tedious to cross. The road has been mostly obliterated, and crossing the wash's multiple rocky ridges and troughs can be rough. Once through the wash, the road begins its ascent, climbing an alluvial fan to the base of the mountain. The scope of the

Collapsed mine entrance with ladder.

operation is clearly visible at this point, with the road, water towers, mine tailings, and other debris stretching nearly to the top of the mountain. At the bottom of the canyon is the mine's base camp, the first of many interesting things to see. Several collapsed wood structures can be found here, as well as stone walls, discarded equipment, trash heaps, and other mine detritus.

From here, the road/trail gets very steep and rugged. About mid-way up the canyon is the first group of mines. A beautiful tin ore bin is the most obvious sight here. Several sealed vertical mine shafts lead into the mountain's depths from this level, their old and broken ladders still visible trailing down into the darkness. Back on the road (one has to ponder how those old cars made it up something so steep), continue onward and upward, eventually reaching a steep wash intersection and crossing. The final leg of the road/trail is possibly the most rugged part of the journey, ascending a steep rocky canyon to the top of the operation, and almost the top of the mountain. At this level, many mine shafts can be found, some sealed, some collapsed, some unsealed. A second beautiful ore bin, this one wood, is perched at the top of the canyon, and a collapsed wooden structure sits out on a dizzying ridge with a commanding view of the canyon and valley below.

For those who still haven't had enough, there is a faint trail leaving the

right side of the level area, leading over the summit of the mountain saddle, and down the back to a couple more shafts.

Details: Park roadside between two small volcanic hills that are just south of Pinto Basin Road, 0.3 miles west of the Cholla Cactus Garden at the west end of Pinto Basin. The mine can be seen on the distant mountain to the south, inside a canyon. Walk between the two small hills, locating an old and faint road that also travels between the hills. Walk the road as it meanders southward toward the mountains. There are several other faint old roads intersecting the road to the mine; just stay on the one that heads more or less straight toward the mine. After approximately 1.5 miles, look for a wash, spot the road on the hillsde opposite, and beeline toward it. There may or may not be cairns denoting a route through the wash. Once across, continue up the road for several hundred yards to a plateau of sorts at the bottom of the canyon. This is where the base camp is located. Continue on the obvious road that heads steeply into the canyon. At the first wash crossing the road is washed out, so pick your way past the washout. As of writing, there was a path on the right side. The first group of mine shafts and machinery will be about 200 yards past this wash. A second wash will be encountered after another 200 yards. Continue on the road, which travels up the smaller left wash, for another 150 yards to the final tier of mines and machinery.

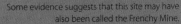
Some evidence suggests that this site may have also been called the Frenchy Mine.

Teddy Bear Cholla cactus as far as the eye can see at the Cholla Cactus Garden.

CHOLLA CACTUS GARDEN

The Cholla Cactus Garden is one of the more interesting sights in Joshua Tree National Park. The very large and dense patch of Teddy Bear Chollas grows on the western slope of Pinto Basin, entrenched in deep alluvial sands. The dark patch of the garden can be seen from many miles away. A paved parking lot and a well-manicured 0.25-mile nature path offers access to this beautiful, albeit somewhat daunting, desert landscape. Informational pamphlets can be found at the start of the path, with interesting facts about the various sights and numbered signposts found along the walkway. Mornings or afternoons are the best times to visit the garden, when the sun is low on the horizon. It is during these times that the sun lights up the furry spines covering the cholla arms, creating a magical, diffuse glow around the cacti.

Many of the cholla found here are large and old, standing 6 feet or more and oftentimes slumped over from their massive arsenal of needles. A few even droop over the path's wooden fences, waiting patiently for unsuspecting sightseers to wander too close!

Photography notes:
The cholla patch is an irresistable location! The strange shapes and foreboding figures of the cacti fit in perfectly with the odd beauty of Joshua Tree National Park. The play of light on the chollas' bright spines combined with the dark undergrowth create a rich pallette of tones and shading, as well as a wide variety of compositional possibilities. Visit the area when the sun is low on the horizon to capture the chollas with a stunning diffuse glow, the sunlight scattering off of the cacti's furry spines, creating bright halos as far as the eye can see.

The Ocotillo Patch is also worth a stop. Though the growth is not nearly as dense as the Cholla Cactus Garden, the ocotillos here are quite large and stately, standing tall with the whole of Pinto Basin stretched out beyond them.

OCOTILLO PATCH

Approximately 1.5 miles east of the Cholla Cactus Garden is this curiosity unique to Pinto Basin. The Ocotillo Patch consists of about 50 ocotillos scattered loosely around a 100-yard patch of gravelly wash and alluvium. Many of the cactus "trees" are quite tall, with some reaching 20 feet or more into the air. A small turnout with an interpretive sign marks the spot.

TURKEY FLATS

As the road makes its way across the vast expanse of Pinto Basin, it passes by an area of the Park known

The spindly arms of an ocotillo, with spring leaves.

as Turkey Flats. This part of the basin is one of the lowest points in Joshua Tree National Park. The merciless exposure and high winds in Turkey Flats creates a barren and forbidding landscape—a textbook desert! There's not much to see here for the casual visitor, but the area is a corridor for backpackers heading up to Pinto Mountain, one of the tallest in the Park and a popular two-day outing. (The hike is beyond the scope of this book.) There are some interesting stabilized sand dunes to be found a mile north of the parking area. Sidewinder snakes, scorpions, and tarantulas are known to frequent the dunes.

     A large parking turnout with a Backcountry Board for the Turkey Flats area can be found 6.1 miles east of the Cholla Cactus Garden on Pinto Basin Road. Conversely, this point is 13.6 miles along the road north of the Cottonwood visitors center.

PORCUPINE WASH

Porcupine Wash is another portal into the backcountry of Joshua Tree National Park, and several multi-day backpacking adventures start here. None of the hikes are short enough to be considered for this book, but they are briefly described on the Backcountry Board that can be found at the parking lot for the area. For those looking for more information on these long hikes, there are several hike-dedicated guidebooks available.

For the day-wanderer, Porcupine Wash offers a pleasant place to roam about and explore. Beautiful smoke trees line the wash, taking on the usual strange contorted shapes that so many other varieties of the Park's "trees" assume. Nearby rocky hills hide faint signs of Native American occupation. Tarantulas and sidewinders occasionally traverse the hard-packed sand.

The parking lot for Porcupine Flats is located 11.2 miles east of the Cholla Cactus Garden on Pinto Basin Road, or 8.4 miles north of the Cottonwood visitors center.

OLD DALE ROAD AND BLACK EAGLE ROAD

Smack-dab in the middle of Pinto Basin on Pinto Basin Road is a dirt road branching off to the north. This road immediately forks into two, Old Dale Road and Black Eagle Road, which both lead off into recent mining districts. There is much to be seen here for those interested in abandoned mines and mining equipment. Mining began in this area in the 1880s, continuing on until the early 1990s when Joshua Tree was elevated to National Park status and its borders were expanded to include the Old Dale and and a portion of the Black Eagle mining districts. In its heyday, the pop-up town of Old Dale was said to have a population of 1000 people.

Both roads are quite popular with 4x4 enthusiasts. Although it's possible to drive these two roads across the flats of Pinto Basin in a low-clearance vehicle, it's not recommended, mostly due to sections of deep sand. These roads lead into some of the most remote locations in the Park. Traveling them alone or in hotter seasons is highly discouraged; visitors have become stranded in this area in the deadly summer heat, perishing before they could reach Pinto Basin Road.

Information board at the turnoff for Old Dale and Black Eagle roads.

Old Dale Road heads north across Pinto Basin, passing Mission Well and the Mission Well Mill site, 10 miles across the broad expanse. Not much to see at Mission Well, just an old pump, an old arrastra, and a small open hole that penetrates some 500 feet into the earth. The well was the lifeblood of the area, providing water for a majority of the basin's occupants. The mill site, located on a small hill on the left side of the road, has several interesting items, including concrete foundations, metal bins, a huge trash heap, and also an unusual turret-shaped foundation of stone. From here the road winds into the rugged mountains, passing many abandoned claims on its steep, rocky path out to Highway 62.

Black Eagle Road travels northeast, and then due east, traversing rolling hills of desert pavement and crossing several rutted washes before heading into the rugged canyon pass at Black Eagle Mine. The road is blocked just before entering the mine. Black Eagle Mine is a large-scale operation located just outside Park boundaries, currently closed, with no mining taking place. Many smaller claims can be found scattered about in the hills and deep canyons around Black Eagle, with names such as Mystery, Storm Jade, and Gypsy. These remote mining locations are not covered in this book, but a bit of sleuthing on the internet can uncover information about them.

The Mission Well site is easily overlooked: There is no designated parking area and bushes have overgrown the entrance.

195

Old stove at an abandoned homestead somewhere on the open plains of Pinto Basin.

The Legend of Storm Jade Mine:

Joshua Tree National Park has an odd pull on the world; it's a sort of vortex attracting all things strange. The Storm Jade story may be one of the strangest. It begins with John G. Climenson, born in Washington, D.C., in 1910. John made his way out west as a young dandy, ending up in Phoenix, Arizona, where the Superstition Mountains captured his interest. He became fascinated with mining lore, eventually writing a book about the treasure of the Lost Dutchman, a famous legend of the Superstitions. Shortly thereafter, John G. Climenson took the name Barry Storm. Storm went on to write several more books, one of which became the basis for a Hollywood production, "Lust for Gold." Storm also wrote occasional articles for Desert Magazine, becoming famous for his tales of legend and lore in the American Southwest.

Storm eventually found himself in the vicinity of what is now Joshua Tree National Park, searching for a lost gold mine and a new legend to chase. As the story goes, while wandering the hills of the Black Eagle, he saw several alien spaceships flying in the sky, one of which shone a beam of light down onto the ground. Taking that as a sign, he searched the spot, and shortly thereafter struck a jade pocket. Storm spent the next 13 years of his life living and working at the site, reportedly removing a single 400-pound chunk of jade. Given the relatively shallow depth of the mine, the question arises as to what exactly he was doing with all his time out there.

Storm believed he had found Mayan beads near the jade pocket, and became obsessed with the notion that the Mayans had traveled to this location to acquire their ceremonial jade—a considerable distance from their homeland in Central America. No one even bothered to verify the authenticity of the beads, and Storm's final adventure never quite panned out for him; his larger-than-life claims were dismissed as the crazy ramblings of a desert wanderer. Isolation, the dessicating heat, and the odd pull of Joshua Tree finally drew him into its fold.

4X4 TRAIL

Old Dale Road

Total distance: 24.5 miles
Difficulties: steep, rocky, rutted road for one
5-mile stretch.
Navigating: 3

Old Dale Road is a popular 4x4 trail that leads
out of the Park. It travels through one of
the most used (and abused) historic mining
districts in the region. Abandoned mines
and equipment lie around every bend. The
road itself is mostly easy driving, with the
exception of several steep, rocky, and rutted
sections ascending into the Pinto Mountains.

The 4x4 trail starts out as just a dirt
road, nearly straight as an arrow across the
expansive flats of Pinto Basin. Several sections
of deep sand keep most passenger cars out.
Once at the far north end of Pinto Basin,
Old Dale Road passes between the Mission
Well and the Mission Well Mill Site, the latter
identified by a large round metal bin sitting a
bit off-kilter on the hillside. Shortly thereafter
the road begins its climb into the rocky Pinto
Mountains. Mines and equipment dot the
hillsides, with spur roads leading every this
way and that. From this point on the road
really begins to climb, becoming rutted and
rocky for several miles as it winds its way
through the hills. Eventually the road will drop
down out of the rocks and onto flat dirt. From
here on out the driving is easy, with only the
occasional rut and dry wash crossing. Keep in

Top: Explosives storeroom at an unknown mine on Old Dale.
Middle: Mother of all refuse heaps at Mission Mill Site.

mind that there are a multitude of roads leading off to mining operations in the area; several
of the larger ones go all the way to Highway 62. Old Dale Road actually turns into Gold Crown
Road, but there aren't any road signs out there anyway. Also note that once outside of Park
boundaries, there may be active mines in the area.

Details: The turnoff to Old Dale Road is on Pinto Basin Road, 22.5 miles southeast of the Pinto
Wye (near the North Entrance), or 7 miles north of Cottonwood visitors center. Turn onto
the dirt road and immediately fork left onto Old Dale Road. Continue across the flats for 10
miles to the Mission Well (on the right) and the Mission Well Mill (on left). Shortly thereafter
the road ascends into the mountains. After about 4 miles, the road will drop down out of
the rocky portion of the hills and into easy terrain. Some navigating may be required from
here on out, as there are many roads leading to various mines: Just stay on the largest road
with the most signs of traffic. Several of the larger roads all lead out to the highway. Once at
Highway 62, turn left (W) to head back to the towns of 29 Palms and Joshua Tree.

Mature cottonwoods and California fan palms thrive in the reliable water of Cottonwood Spring.

CHAPTER 8
SOUTH ENTRANCE

Visitors coming in by way of Arizona on Interstate 10 or from the lower Coachella Valley will want to enter the Park from the South Entrance. This side of the Park is somewhat removed from the signature Mojave side of Joshua Tree National Park, with its towering rock piles and, well, Joshua trees. Visitors from this side will be greeted by barren mountains, deep sandy canyons, spindley ocotillo, and scraggly smoke trees—a very different place than the "other" side of the park. This is Sonoran Desert at its finest, with all the typical plants and cactus that cover much of the American Southwest. But not a Joshua tree to be seen for many miles!

Several classic desert oases can be found here, with splashes of inviting green foliage tucked away at the mouths of prominent canyons. Here visitors can truly appreciate these small patches of Eden, enjoying rare shade, pleasant birdsong, and the soothing rustle of leaves blowing in the breeze.

Historical mine sites are also prevalent on this side of Joshua Tree. The area's highly mineralized mountains were once the stuff of many a '49er's dream. The nearby and reliable oases were also a contributing factor in the development of mining in this area. Not only was the precious water a necessity for survival in this harsh world, it was also crucial in the processing of the ores that were extracted.

After exiting Interstate 10, the entrance road, National Park Drive, travels north, gently rising up the slope of a broad alluvial fan on its way toward a large canyon serving as a portal to the enclosed valleys of Joshua Tree National Park. Just before the Park boundary is a stretch of BLM land that is popular with campers. The first point of interest after entering the Park is the Bajada Trail, a short nature walk with interpretive signage discussing alluvial fans, bajadas, and their place in the desert ecosystem. The trail is wheelchair accessible and has accomodations for the visually impaired. Further along, the road steepens and enters a large wash and canyon, becoming quite winding as it makes its way through the pass. Watch for oncoming traffic here; drivers coming down the pass build excessive speed and seem to have a tendency to cross the double yellow line! Once you're through the pass, the Cottonwood Visitors Center will come into view. The paved

Smoke tree growing in Smoke Tree Wash.

Smoke Tree Wash

to Smoke Tree Wash Parking, Pinto Basin

Pinkham Canyon 4x4 Road

Pinto Basin Road

Pinkham Canyon Road

Cottonwood

Cottonwood Spring Road

Lost Palms Oasis Trail

Lost Palms Oasis **41**

SOUTH ENTRANCE

Bajada Trail **39**

parking

Park Entrance

Cottonwood Springs Road

10

N

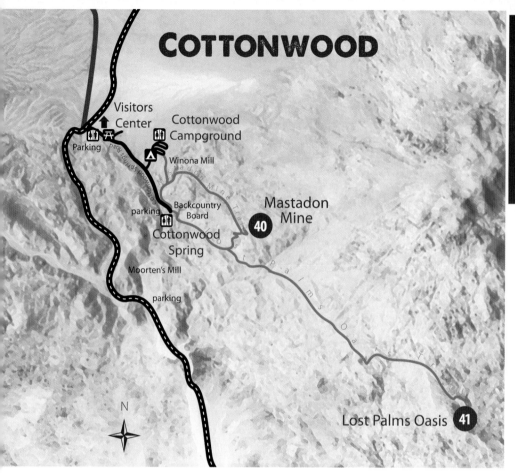

COTTONWOOD

Visitors Center

Parking

Cottonwood Campground

Winona Mill

parking

Backcountry Board

Cottonwood Spring

Moorten's Mill

parking

Mastadon Mine **40**

Lost Palms Oasis **41**

N

road on the right (E) is Cottonwood Spring Road. National Park Drive turns into Pinto Basin Road at this point. The Cottonwood Spring Road leads to the campground, Cottonwood Spring, and the trailhead for Mastadon Loop and the Lost Palms Oasis. The dirt road on the left (W) is Pinkham Canyon Road.

Back on the main route north, Pinto Basin Road, the views open up to reveal the vast expanse of Pinto Basin in the distance, the terrain alternating between rock-covered hills and wide-open desert, punctuated by large washes that drain into Pinto Basin. One of the largest drainages in the area, Smoke Tree Wash, is a beautiful place to get out and just roam across the open desert. The sand is usually packed solid, making the travel akin to walking down a 10-lane freeway but with beautiful pale blue-grey smoke trees crowding its lanes instead of vehicles.

Bajada Trail - #39

Total distance: 0.3-mile loop
Physical difficulty: 1
Technical difficulty: 1
Navigating: 1
Trail type: official, wheelchair-accessible

Wash crossing at the entrance to the Bajada Trail.

The Bajada Trail is a short nature walk meandering across a prominent bajada that skirts the mountain range at the South Entrance. A bajada is a conjoining series of alluvial fans, the accumulated debris runoff from mountain canyons. Alluvial fans often grow so large that they merge into each other, forming a bajada along the base of entire mountain ranges. This geological feature is common in mature deserts, and the bajada at the South Entrance of Joshua Tree is an exceptional example. Interpretive signs go into further detail, as well as describing the local flora and its relationship with this Colorado Desert Bajada ecosystem.

The trail is not paved, but is wheelchair accessible, accomodates visually impaired trekkers, and has several rest benches along the way. Incidentally, the building of this trail was filmed for an episode of Huell Howser's "California Gold."

Details: The turnoff for the Bajada Trail is located 1.4 miles north of Interstate 10 on National Park Drive (0.5 miles from the Park boundary) on the road's east side. A large interpretive sign marks the start of the walk and features a map of the trail.

COTTONWOOD VISITORS CENTER

The Cottonwood Visitors Center is located just north of Cottonwood Spring Road on National Park Drive. The visitors center has all of the typical amenities: information, brochures, a book store, running water, and real flushable toilets! A nearby paved nature walk gives visitors a glimpse of the local terrain, with interpretive signs giving the names and information on plants seen along the way.

COTTONWOOD CAMPGROUND

Cottonwood Campground is the only campground on the entire eastern side of Joshua Tree National Park. It's also one of the only two campgrounds in the entire Park that has running water. The grounds, situated on the edge of the open plains, offer 61 individual sites and 3 group sites scattered among a desert forest of creosote, yucca, and ironwood. Craggy hills and mountains form the backdrop. Just about every area of interest on this side of the Park can be accessed on foot from the campground, including the visitors center, the botanical walk, the Winona Mill, Cottonwood Spring, Mastadon Loop, and even the Lost Palms Oasis.

　　　　The campground is located behind the Cottonwood Visitors Center. Turn east onto Cottonwood Spring Road, drive 0.7 miles and turn left into the campground. A fee kiosk can be found near the entrance. Individual sites are on a first-come, first-served basis. The group sites require reservations.

Oases in this part of the Park are the real deal! Lush overgrowth and undergrowth provide shade and shelter for birds, animals, and parched visitors looking for respite from the elements. Precious surface water can also be found here.

COTTONWOOD SPRING

Cottonwood Spring is an amazing sight in this withered and barren land. Lush green cottonwood and palm trees tower above dense thickets of screwbean mesquite growing along a sandy wash. The intoxicating sound of trickling water can be heard from deep within the tangle of foliage. Cottonwood Spring has been the lifeblood of this region for untold generations for both wildlife and humans.

Cahuilla Indians lived here and used the spring for hundreds of years. One can imagine what a paradise this must have been for them—the running water, the shade trees, the abundance of plants and wildlife. Two matates, ground into a rock lying on the bank of the wash, are the only reminder of the Cahuilla's longtime harmonious coexistence with this place.

The spring later became an important portal for travel and mining in the valleys and mountains beyond. Local miners also relied on the water to process their ore, with several gold mines sprouting up in the vicinity of the spring.

Todays visitors can reach the spring via a 50-yard paved walkway leading from the parking lot. Park benches invite guests to sit under the shade of the trees, watch for exotic birds, and listen to the entrancing rustle of cottonwood leaves and palm fronds blowing in the breeze. Interpretive signs in the area describe plants and the native uses for them.

From Pinto Basin Road/National Park Drive, turn east onto Cottonwood Spring Road and drive 1.1 miles to the end parking. Restrooms and a Backcountry Board can be found here. The beautiful spring and wash can be viewed from the parking lot. The walk leading down to the spring is located behind the Backcountry Board. This walk is also the launch point for the Mastadon Loop and the Lost Palms Oasis.

HIKE

Mastadon Mine - #40

Total distance: 2.2 miles (loop)
Physical difficulty: 3
Technical difficulty: 2
Navigating: 1
Trail type: official trail

The elaborate mine entrance and ore chute. The structure has undergone several restorations to help stabilize old and rotting wood beams.

Mastadon Mine is located high on a rocky hillside below the summit of Mastadon Peak. The site has a fascinating wood structure that is very well preserved (save for several rotted posts that were recently replaced by the Park Service to prevent the structure from collapsing). All of the typical mining debris can be found scattered in a wash below the mine: wood, steel drums, pipes, tin cans, and even an arrastra wheel. There was reportedly a wood

office structure and a ball mill on location, but time has pretty much obliterated them both. The mine site offers stellar views of distant landscapes, including the Salton Sea and even Signal Hill in Mexico.

The gold mine, owned by a George W. Hulsey of Indio, was in full operation

204

A blooming ocotillo and stunning views of the Oricopa Mountains as seen from the trail to the Lost Palms Oasis.

from 1919 to 1932. The family continued to work the mine until the early 1970s, when the mine was acquired by the Park Service.

Details: Park at the Backcountry Board at the end of Cottonwood Spring Road. Take the walkway down to Cottonwood Spring, then continue on the large and well-worn trail traveling east. Signposts mark the trail the whole way. The trail will rise over a hill, drop down on stairs and back into a wash, then rise again onto a hill. At 0.7 miles there will be a junction with a sign; heading right leads to Lost Palms Oasis, heading left goes to Mastadon Peak and the Mastadon Mine.

From here the trail rises steeply, winding into the rocky hillside and on to Mastadon Peak. A flat area will be encountered below the peak. To reach the peak, switchback right and continue uphill to the back side of the peak, where a short scramble up rocks leads to the true summit.

To continue on to the mine, follow the trail across the flat area (you will now be traveling northwest). The mine will become visible, with the trail dropping down between the main shaft and a wood structure. From the mine, the trail runs along a ridge before dropping down off the mountain and into a sandy wash. Follow the wash northwest, passing through a constriction in the rocks, then more open wash. The trail will exit the wash on its right side, continuing over a small hill before dropping into a second wash. Follow this wash as it bends to the left, heading back to Cottonwood Spring Road about 0.1 miles west of the parking area. Just before the road, look for the botanical trail which extends out into this area on the left. Take this trail to avoid the road, or just walk the road, turning left back to the parking lot.

HIKE
Lost Palms Oasis - #41

Total distance: 6.4 miles (round trip)
Physical difficulty: 4
Technical difficulty: 3
Navigating: 2
Trail type: official trail

The Lost Palms Oasis is a beautiful desert oasis tucked deep in a rugged canyon, located on the far southeastern edge of the Joshua Tree plateau. With over 100 palms, it is the largest California Fan Palm oasis in the Park. The splash of lush green foliage in this harsh arid land is invigorating. The rustling of the leaves, birdsong echoing through the canyon, and inviting shade make this a true paradise. A second dense stand of palms grows in a valley hanging high above the canyon floor.

LOST PALMS CANYON
THIS CANYON CONTAINS THE LARGEST GROUP OF CALIFORNIA FAN PALMS IN THE PARK

The hike out to Lost Palm Oasis is tougher than you might expect. The trail covers rugged terrain, repeatedly dropping into and then climbing out of washes. As the hike progresses, the washes just get deeper and deeper! Navigating is easy, though, as the trail is well marked and well worn for its entirety.

(continue)

The stately fan palms at the Lost Palms Oasis. A second stand of palms can be seen high in the canyon to the left.

Top: Ocotillo dominate the landscape in this area of the Park. This patch of blooms was photographed from the trail.
Middle: NPS sign marking the "secret" path through a dense stand of desert willow trees—just one of the many unique sights along the journey.

(continued)

The journey is a beautiful one. Beginning with the stroll through Cottonwood Spring and its greenery, the towering palms just a taste of the sights ahead. From here, the trail rises to a high plain, and then onto another. The high plains in this corner of the Park are bisected by many (and I do mean many!) washes draining out into the low desert beyond the plateau. The rolling terrain starts out gently, crossing broad washes with creosote and thickets of willow, and then along low hilltops with occasional stunning vistas of the Salton Sea, the Orocopia Mountains, and even the Colorado River area. Further along, the trail begins to lose elevation, dropping down into steep corridors and canyons, then again rising along rocky hillsides to meander atop ridges before dropping into the next canyon. Eventually the trail will rise to follow a ridge, turn a bend, and there will be the Lost Palms Oasis sign. The main oasis is barely visible down in the canyon below. Visitors can either walk out along the ridge for a better view or take a steep and loose trail down to the canyon floor and the oasis. Down at the oasis, a sandy wash meanders under the palm trees and through thick brush.

Details: Park at the Backcountry Board at the end of Cottonwood Spring Road. Take the walkway down to Cottonwood Spring, then continue on the large and well-worn trail traveling east. Signposts mark the trail the whole way. The trail will rise over a hill, drop down on stairs and back into a wash, then rise again onto a hill. At 0.7 miles there will be a junction with signs: Heading left goes to Mastadon Peak and the Mastadon Mine; take the right fork and head to Lost Palms Oasis.

The trail will meander through rolling hills for a bit and then cross several large, sandy washes, one featuring a dense stand of willow trees with the trail tunneling through. Eventually the trail will reach the edge of the Joshua Tree plateau, with steep canyons dropping off to the south and east. The trail drops into one of these. The first canyon is like a thin corridor, with steep cliffs rising on both sides. The climb out is short but burly, with a bit of easier ridge walking in between so you can regain your composure before dropping into the next canyon. The second significant canyon starts with a steep drop on loose terrain. The canyon runs for about 0.25 miles, heading east and ending in some truly rugged terrain. Gain one final ridge summit and the lookout should come into view, with the upper palm oasis clearly visible high in an adjacent canyon. The main oasis is in the canyon below.

To reach a better vantage point, walk out and along the ridge above the palms. Use extreme caution as there are 100-foot cliffs below the ridge, and slipping here could result in death. Also take care not to dislodge rocks onto people who may be in the canyon below. To get down to the palms, take the very steep and slippery trail leading down the hill behind the sign. From here it is also possible to scramble up to the higher set of fan palms in the canyon above.

Top: An unusual brown-blooming silver cholla.
Middle: A blooming ocatillo stands high above a rugged canyon, catching the last rays of daylight. Beyond the canyon, a 100-mile view goes as far as the Colorado River and even into Arizona.

4X4 TRAIL

Pinkham Canyon Road

Total distance: 20 miles
Difficulties: washboard roads, deep sand for second half
Navigating: 2

Pinkham Canyon Road is a moderate to easy 4x4 road that travels into the remote Cottonwood Mountains that form the southern border of the Joshua Tree high plateau. The road passes through beautiful pristine Colorado Desert landscape, across broad alluvial fans, through massive washes, and down steep, rocky canyons on its way to Interstate 10 in the lower desert to the south.

Details: The start of Pinkham Canyon Road is located across from the Cottonwood Visitors Center on Pinto Basin Road. Turn north here. The road starts out with a bit of deep sand, intermittently traveling through and alongside washes for 1 mile before cutting across a broad alluvial fan, where driving conditions firm up. The road then veers to the left, traveling westward into a broad valley containing the beautiful Smoke Tree Wash. After about 6.5 miles the road conquers a small hill before dropping down into an adjacent canyon with a large, sandy wash. This deep canyon snakes its way east for 5.2 miles to a junction with another 4x4 road called Thermal Canyon. Not as scenic as Pinkham Canyon, this side road, on the right,

Thunderheads brewing over the nearby Salton Sea, a common sight in late summer along Pinkham Canyon Road.

adds 4 miles and leads to the same general location near the freeway. A sign should mark the junction but it may have washed away. At this point Pinkham Canyon/Road hairpins to the left, traveling east and then bending back to the south, curving its way into an even deeper canyon for 3 more miles, eventually opening up onto a broad alluvial fan. Drive for 3.5 miles to a junction with Aqueduct Road. Turn left (E) onto pavement and drive 3 miles to the on ramp for Interstate 10.

The information board at the beginning of the Pinkham Canyon Road.

CHAPTER 9
ALONG HIGHWAY 62

A standing graveyard of burned piñon pines creates an eerie scene at Covington Flats. Fires ravaged this area 20 years ago.

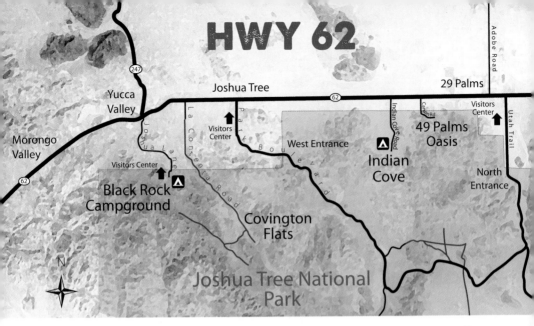

ALONG HIGHWAY 62

Highway 62 traverses the entire length of Joshua Tree National Park. To the west, beginning in Coachella Valley near the famous windmills of Palm Springs, the highway wraps around the western tip of the Park, skirting its northern border to its eastern terminus, some 100 miles distant. Along this stretch there are several roads leading to isolated sections of the Park. These include Black Rock Campground, Covington Flats, Indian Cove, and the 49 Palms Oasis.

This spread of areas covers the full gambit of Joshua Tree terrain: lush juniper and piñon pine forests in the Mojave high country of Black Rock, mature Joshua tree forests (some being the largest in the Park) at Covington Flats, massive rock piles at Indian Cove, and a classic Lower Colorado Desert oasis at 49 Palms Oasis. Two of the largest campgrounds in Joshua Tree National Park are located along Highway 62: Black Rock and Indian Cove.

The highway passes through five towns during its west-to-east rally across the desert. At the Park's western border is Desert Hot Springs, known for its mineral hot springs and spas. Next is the quaint little town of Morongo Valley. Check out the beautiful Morongo Preserve if time permits, located near the center of town. The third and largest town is Yucca Valley. Approaching city status, Yucca Valley is the shopping hub for this entire side of the high desert. All the amenities can be found here: grocery stores, resturaunts, fast food, gas stations, hotels, big chain stores, and trendy coffeehouses. Next is the town of Joshua Tree, the main portal for Joshua Tree National Park, via its West Entrance. Many small mom-and-pop stores, art stores, and restaurants can be found at the town center. The easternmost town is 29 Palms. This town is fairly small, but the nearby 29 Palms Marine Base fuels a strong local market, enabling sizeable hotels and a variety of stores to thrive. 29 Palms is also the portal for the North Entrance to Joshua Tree National Park.

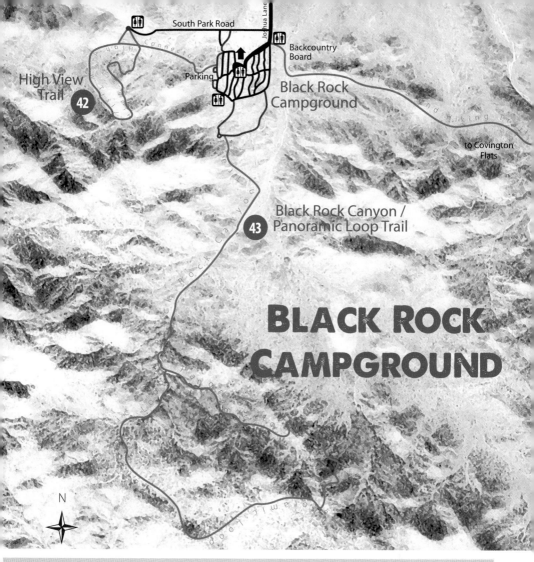

South Park Road

Joshua Lane

Backcountry Board

High View Trail **42**

Parking

Black Rock Campground

to Covington Flats

Black Rock Canyon / Panoramic Loop Trail **43**

BLACK ROCK CAMPGROUND

N

INTO ART?

The towns of 29 Palms, Joshua Tree, and Yucca Valley have a thriving local art scene. Several galleries can be found in the vicinity, and many other businesses display the work of local artists. The area is also home to the Highwayy 62 Art Tours, a regional event where local artists open their home studios for the general public to visit and view art. Note that most galleries are only open on Friday, Saturday, and Sunday. Call or check gallery websites for business hours and information.

29 Palms Art Gallery. This is the largest and oldest of the local galleries. Adobe architecture gives the museum a historical feel. It is also just a stone's throw away from the Joshua Tree Visitors Center in 29 Palms. 74055 Cottonwood Dr, 29 Palms; (760) 367-7819, 29palmsartgallery.com.

29 Palms Creative Center and Art Gallery. This center displays art from local artists, as well as offering a wide variety of art activities and classes for people of all ages. Great for children! 6847 Adobe Road, 29 Palms; (760) 361-1805, 29palmsart.com.

(continue)

(continued)

The Glass Outhouse Art Gallery. A small gallery situated on a grounds filled with eclectic and quirky displays. Visitors can roam about and explore, as well as peruse art from local artists. 77575 State Highway 62, 29 Palms; (760) 367-3807.

Gallery 62. A small gallery located near the hub of the town of Joshua Tree's social scene, Park Boulevard and Hwy 62. Visitors can park here and roam on foot, perusing art at the gallery before walking to nearby gift stores, restaurants, bars, markets, and the Joshua Tree Visitors Center. 61607 State Highway 62, Joshua Tree; www.hwy62art.org.

Joshua Tree Art Gallery. This fine gallery is also located near the Park Boulevard/Hwy 62 social hub. Visitors here can park the car, check out the gallery, then wander past cafés, restaurants, and small stores. 61607 State Highway 62, Joshua Tree; (760) 366-3636, www.joshuatreeartgallery.com.

Hwy 62 Art Tours. This is a 2-weekend event that happens in the fall. Local artists from Morongo Valley, Yucca Valley, Joshua Tree, and 29 Palms open their homes and studios to the public. Visitors get to meet the artists and see where the art is created, as well as view and purchase their works. See the website for details on this excellent event. www.hwy62arttours.org.

BLACK ROCK CAMPGROUND

Aside from being one of the largest campgrounds in Joshua Tree National Park, Black Rock Campground is also one of most modern, with 101 sites, water close by, RV accommodations, horse accommodation sites, and the Black Rock Visitors Center. The visitors center has staff on hand for assistance and information, plus displays and a gift shop. The campground is also just a skip away from the middle of the town of Yucca Valley, with grocery stores, sporting goods, resturaunts, and even fast food a mere 5 miles distant!

Several interesting hikes can be found here, including the initial section of the California Riding and Hiking Trail. This trail travels east through the Park for 32 miles before turning north and exiting near the North Entrance at 29 Palms. Other nearby hikes include the High View Trail, which travels through the area's rugged hills to a summit with dramatic views of the surrounding mountains and valleys. Many other hikes in the 6- to 10-mile range can be found in this area that are not covered in this book. For more information on these hikes, acquire a map brochure from the visitors center.

The "official" route into Black Rock, posted with signs, is to take Joshua Lane south from Highway 62 in Yucca Valley, traveling somewhat roundabout for 5 miles to the campground. A more direct route is to take Avalon Avenue (which soon becomes Palomar) south from just west of the Super Walmart, at the east end of town. After 3 miles, Palomar ends at Joshua Lane. Continue south on Joshua Lane for another mile to its end at the campground.

The grandaddy of all nolinas can be seen on the High View Trail, as well as many other old-growth trees and desert flora.

A hard-earned rest bench with a grand view, found at the midpoint of the High View Trail.

HIKE

High View Trail - #42

Total distance: 2-mile loop (from Black Rock)
Physical difficulty: 2
Technical difficulty: 2
Navigating: 1
Trail type: official trail

This fine trail roams a short distance across the chaparral high country of Black Rock Canyon before ascending steeply to a dramatic hilltop. The hilltop has a climbing register and a bench on which to rest and take in the wide vistas of the surrounding mountains and valleys, as well as the town of Yucca Valley. Beautiful old yuccas, dwarf junipers, gnarled scrub oak, and bonsai piñon pines adorn the steep slopes of the hills. Past the summit, the trail winds its way down the back of the hill, where you finally exit via a quiet canyon thick in Joshua trees and turbinella oak. Incidentally, there is a High View Trail brochure (available for free at the ranger station), which gives information on plants and animal habitation seen at numbered markers along the trail.

Details: This hike has two possible starting points. The shorter version begins outside the National Park, at the adjoining South Park, at the end of South Park Road. From here, the total hike distance is 1.3 miles. Alternatively, start from the northwest side of the Black Rock Campground. See map on page 215. The following description is for the latter, starting within the Park boundaries.

Park at the trailhead parking on the northwest side of Black Rock Campground. Take the trail, also marked as West Loop, rising over a low ridge, down a gully, and then onto relatively flat ground. At 0.5 miles the trail will intersect another trail. Take a left, marked as High View, and follow the trail southward. Shortly thereafter, the trail will begin its ascent. About two-thirds of the way up, a scenic bench will be found. A final steep dash leads to the climbing register, another rest bench, and the official highpoint of the trail. A short spur trail leads to the true summit. From here the trail makes its way down the back of the hill and back to flat ground, curving around the base of the hills to return to the parking lot. Two trail junctions will be encountered: Turning left at either one will lead to the South Park parking lot. Continue straight ahead for the trailhead in Black Rock Campground.

HIKE

Black Rock Canyon with Panoramic Loop - #43

Total distance: 5.5 miles
Physical difficulty: 3
Technical difficulty: 1
Navigating: 2
Trail type: official trail

The Black Rock Canyon Panoramic Loop is a trail with a dual personality. The majority of it travels uneventfully up a wash and through a small canyon, with nary a big view in sight! It's not until the very end of the journey that the trail rises steeply onto the mountainside, traversing exposed ridges and crests to reach a dramatic summit with incredible views in all directions. This summit has that top-of-the-world feel to it, with the high country of Joshua Tree National Park dropping off to the north, west, and south for many thousands of feet. The return trip

Above: Living up to its name, the Panoramic Loop has big views in every direction. In this view to the north, one can see the town of Yucca Valley, Lucerne Valley, and even as far as Barstow.

is downhill for almost its entirety, making for an easy finish.

Details: Park at the Black Rock Visitors Center and walk to the southern end of the campground. A small sign marks the start of the trail, located to the left of a lone campsite at the southern tip of the campground. The sign notes the Panoramic Loop and several other trails. Take the trail, which is actually a faint old road, as it bends to the right (SW) and leads over a hump to a large water tower. Follow the road as it bends to the left (E). The trail can be found to the right just past the bend below the water tower, signposted "West Loop Trail." Take the trail, now heading southeast, for 200 yards to a fork with a sign. The right fork is the West Loop Trail, the left fork is for Panoramic Loop and the other trails. Take the left fork and follow the trail for 400 yards to a sandy

wash. More signage here notes trails. Burnt Hill Trail continues on (E), and the Panoramic Loop (and Warren Peak) heads south up the wash. Turn right and head south up the sandy wash. Continue in the main wash as it slowly becomes a small canyon (Black Rock Canyon). Look for Black Rock Spring after 0.8 miles—usually just a damp pit at the base of a rock. A cluster of mesquite grows on the hillside at the spring, as well as other greenery. From the spring, travel another 300 yards to a split in the canyon (and more signs). This is the start (and finish) of the loop portion of the trail. The loop is described here counter-clockwise, so take a left (ESE) at the junction and continue up the slightly smaller side canyon for 0.5 miles. The canyon will get smaller and smaller, disappearing below a tall peak. From here the trail will begin a series of switchbacks as it rises onto the mountain, traveling another 0.7 miles to gain the summit. After the summit, the trail descends to the west, crossing a saddle, then rising briefly to pass behind an adjacent peak. (A faint side trail leads steeply to this summit.) The trail then meanders along ridges, gently descending as it continues west, eventually dropping into a small wash in a valley. The wash curves to the northwest and intersects another wash approximately 1 mile from the summit. A sign here notes the Warren Peak Trail to the left (W), and the Panoramic Loop to the right (N). Head right, which will now be north, "downstream" in Black Rock Canyon. Note the black rocks in this area, from which the canyon gets its name. Continue for another 0.3 miles to the junction in the canyon where the loop started. Take the left fork, retracing your approach now, continuing downhill in the main canyon, past Black Rock Spring and out into the open valley where the wash veers to the northeast. Watch for the signs and turn left onto a trail which leads northwest out of the wash and gently uphill toward the water tower. Once at the service road, turn left and follow the road as it bends to the right and travels over a hump and back to the campground.

The Tree of Tortured Souls in one of the burn areas of Covington Flats. The arms of burned Joshua trees, such as this one, can resemble misshapen bones, and for this reason the area has been dubbed "The Boneyard."

COVINGTON FLATS

to Yucca
Valley,
HWY 62

N

Covington Flats is a large open plain found in the high country of Joshua Tree's far western end. The area is completely undeveloped, with the exception of several dirt roads and trails. The "flats" are typically divided into two areas: Lower Covington Flats and Upper Covington Flats. The first, traversed by Lower Covington Flats Road, is curiously devoid of standing trees, the result of 1999 wildfires that ravaged the area. The ghostly remains of burned Joshua trees litter the desert floor, giving the area a bizzare, almost spooky, look. Upper Covington Flats is a completely different story. Spared from the fires, this area boasts dense stands of juniper and some of the

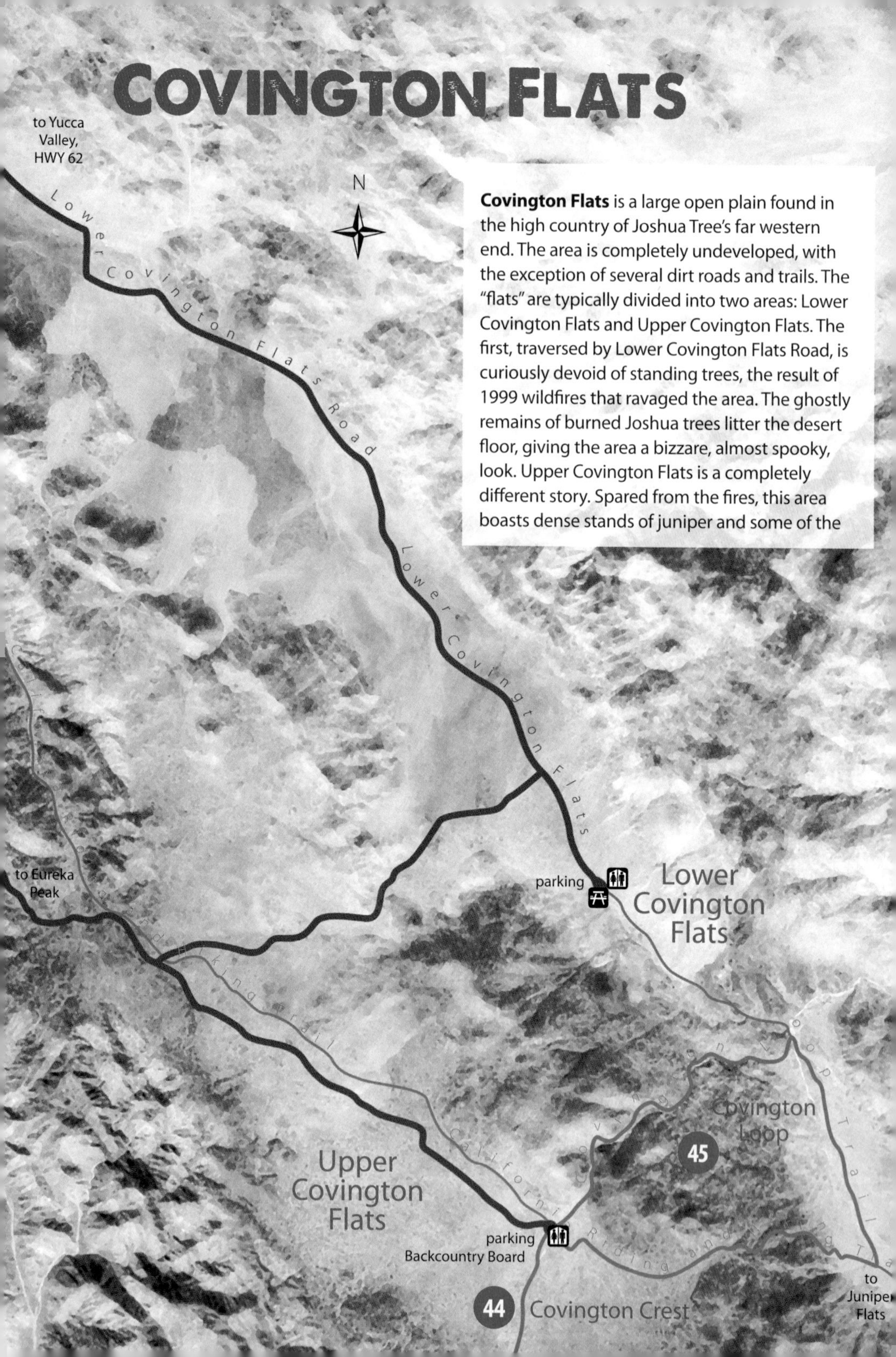

Lower Covington Flats Road

Lower Covington Flats

to Eureka
Peak

parking

Lower
Covington
Flats

Covington
Loop

45

Upper
Covington
Flats

California Riding and Hiking Trail

parking
Backcountry Board

44 Covington Crest

to
Juniper
Flats

largest Joshua trees in the entire Park. Mule deer can sometimes be seen here in the dawn hours. There are several scenic hikes at Upper Covington Flats, and the long California Riding and Hiking Trail passes through the middle of it all.

Covington Flats is located in the hills south of the southern end of Yucca Valley. Sole access to this area is via the dusty, 10-mile-long Lower Covington Flats Road. The road is mildly rutted and has a few sandy spots, but it is usually driveable in a passenger car. From Highway 62, on the east edge of Yucca Valley, turn south onto La Contenta Road. After 1 mile, La Contenta crosses Yucca Trail and turns to dirt. Continue south on La Contenta for another 1.8 miles; veer left here, onto Lower Covington Road. Several ruts and a somewhat sandy section will have to be negotiated. Travel 5.8 miles, passing a Joshua Tree National Park entrance sign, to a junction. Continuing straight at the junction will lead to a dead end at a trailhead and crude picnic area. Turn right (N) at the junction toward the Upper Covington Flats area for the hikes described in this book. Travel southwest for 1.8 miles to another junction. Turn left and follow the road for a final 1.9 miles to a small parking loop. A Backcountry Board and trail signs can be found here. (Turning right at the final junction leads to parking for Eureka Peak, where a steep 150-yard grunt leads to the stunning summit.)

HIKE

Covington Crest - #44

Total distance: 3 miles (round trip)
Physical difficulty: 1
Technical difficulty: 1
Navigating: 1
Trail type: official trail

The view from the edge of Covington Crest. Sights include Palm Springs and most of Coachella Valley, and the Santa Rosa Mountains behind.

The Covington Crest trail may be one of the finest easy hikes in Joshua Tree National Park. Its location in this much less populated section of the Park gives it a remote, untrammeled feel. The trail meanders across the gently rolling flats of Upper Covington, weaving through groves of tall juniper and Joshua trees, ever-so-slightly ascending on its way to the edge of the flats. A rim of jagged rock with rock cairns marks the end of the trail, where the Covington Flats plateau drops away dramatically into a series of deep canyons, eventually draining into the large graben of Coachella Valley. Imagine the mighty San Andreas fault stretching and pulling the valley floor, causing it to sink down, meanwhile tipping massive blocks of crust on both sides to create the Little San Bernardino mountains that you are standing on, along with the Santa Rosas and Mt. San

Jacinto on the opposite side of the valley. A short side trek to the summit of the hill to the west, know as Lone Tree Hill, expands the view to include Mt. San Gorgonio and the San Bernardino Mountains.

Details: Park at the end loop at Upper Covington Flats. To the right of the Backcountry Board is a trailhead noting the Covington Crest Trail. Follow the well-groomed trail as it travels alongside a wash for quite a way, crossing it in several places. Near the end, the juniper stands will get dense and the ground a bit rockier. The trail will end abruptly at a rocky ridge with cairns built on it.

HIKE

Covington Loop - #45

Total distance: 3.5 miles
Physical difficulty: 2
Technical difficulty: 1
Navigating: 2
Trail type: cross-country/wash/trail

The Covington Loop is another fine route located in Upper Covington Flats. This one travels a wider variety of terrain than the Covington Crest Trail, fording deep, sandy canyons, traversing rugged chaparral hills, and roaming the open Covington Flats.

Starting at the Upper Covington trailhead, the initial cross-country section traverses the upper flats, passing some truly huge Joshua tress en route. Soon after, the hike ducks into a deep canyon following a pristine wash that makes its way past rocky impasses and through thick foliage to reach the other side of the canyon in Lower Covington Flats. From here the trail bends back around, this time taking the high ground into the rugged hills separating Lower and Upper Covington. The steeply inclined trail twists and weaves through dwarf juniper and sage forests intermixed with tall yucca, barrel cactus, hedgehog cactus, and beavertail. Rocky ridges along the way offer excellent vistas of Lower Covington Flats and the hills beyond. Once through the hills, the trail drops back onto the "flats," traveling among more large Joshua trees.

the left of the CRH trail is a canyon leading through the hills; the Covington Loop travels through this canyon. Head cross-country to the canyon. Proceed through, walking a sandy wash for 1 mile, to the canyon's end at Lower Covington Flats. Exiting the canyon, the wash intersects a wash going southward. Turn right and follow this wash for approximately 0.8 miles, to where the CRH intersects it. Turn right onto the CRH trail and follow it through the steep hills for another 0.5 miles. The final 0.75 miles is on easy flat ground.

Details: It is possible to hike this trail from either the picnic area in Lower Covington or from the Backcountry Board in Upper Covington—see map on page 222. This description is for the latter. At the Backcountry Board, the California Riding and Hiking Trail leads off to the east (you will return this way). About 45-degrees to

Above: Some of the largest Joshua trees in the Park can be found at Covington Flats, such as this behemoth near the Upper Covington parking lot. The largest recorded Joshua tree had grown here alongside this one; it eventually succumbed to the elements (possibly lightning).

Opposite page: Vibrant wildflowers bloom beneath an old piñon snag.

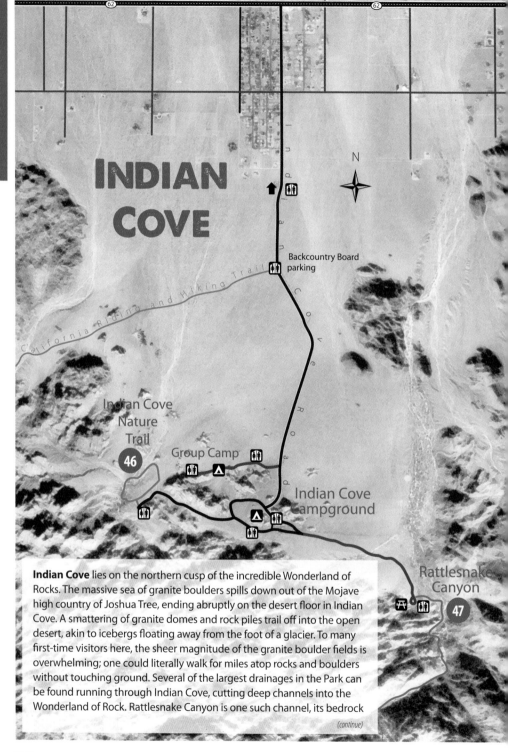

INDIAN COVE

Backcountry Board parking

California Riding and Hiking Trail

N

Indian Cove Road

Indian Cove Nature Trail

46

Group Camp

Indian Cove Campground

Rattlesnake Canyon

47

Indian Cove lies on the northern cusp of the incredible Wonderland of Rocks. The massive sea of granite boulders spills down out of the Mojave high country of Joshua Tree, ending abruptly on the desert floor in Indian Cove. A smattering of granite domes and rock piles trail off into the open desert, akin to icebergs floating away from the foot of a glacier. To many first-time visitors here, the sheer magnitude of the granite boulder fields is overwhelming; one could literally walk for miles atop rocks and boulders without touching ground. Several of the largest drainages in the Park can be found running through Indian Cove, cutting deep channels into the Wonderland of Rock. Rattlesnake Canyon is one such channel, its bedrock

(continue)

scoured and fluted by eons of flash-flooding. The canyon's many potholes, natural tanks, and pools hold water, sometimes year-round, attracting bighorn, mule deer, and other desert critters.

The campground at Indian Cove is the second largest in Joshua Tree National Park with 101 individual sites and 13 group sites, several equipped for RV and equestrian use. All of the sites here are available by reservation, with any unreserved sites available to walk-in campers. A small ranger station is located 2 miles north of the campground entrance, offering water and general information as well as assistance.

Indian Cove offers much for visitors: short hikes, long hikes, picnic areas, endless rock piles to crawl around on, and deep canyons to explore. The Indian Cove Nature Trail is a good introduction to the area, a 0.6-mile loop out across the desert, through a sandy wash, then back. Interpretive signs identify plants along the trail and relate other interesting facts about the desert. Another trail of interest is the Boyscout Trail, which "ends" its 8-mile, one-way trek through the Wonderland of Rocks at Indian Cove. (Most start it from the other side at Quail Springs because of the elevation loss.) For those looking for something a bit less committing, it's possible to walk up just a portion of the lower Boyscout Trail. The trail crosses flat ground for the first mile and a half, before entering a large wash and the canyon that continues into the upper part of Joshua Tree.

Rattlesnake Canyon Picnic Area sits at the foot of the mighty granite boulder piles. If there were a single "best" place in the Park to sit and eat a sandwich, this could be it! Visitors can climb rock piles that rise from directly behind the picnic tables, walk along the margin of the open desert and the rock piles, or even wander up the huge, sandy wash at the mouth of Rattlesnake Canyon. Continuing on into Rattlesnake Canyon is perhaps one of the great hikes in all of Joshua Tree, leading deep into the Wonderland of Rocks.

To get to Indian Cove, take Highway 62 to Indian Cove Road, located 13 miles east of the town of Joshua Tree, 10 miles west of 29 Palms. Take Indian Cove Road south for 1 mile to the Park entrance. The campground is 2 miles farther. For the Rattlesnake Canyon area, veer left at the 3-way intersection just inside the campground, drive 150 yards or so, then veer right. The road will end at another dirt road heading east/west. Turn left and take this road for 1 mile, leaving the campground and traveling to the southeast corner of Indian Cove and the mouth of Rattlesnake Canyon.

HIKE

Indian Cove Nature Trail - #46

Total distance: 0.6 miles (round trip)
Physical difficulty: 1
Technical difficulty: 1
Navigating: 1
Trail type: official trail

The Indian Cove Nature Trail is a short and easy hike that is a great introduction to the desert terrain found around Indian Cove. The trail is well marked, well trodden, and travels with minimal elevation gain on its journey out across the desert and through a large wash. Interpretive signs are found along the path, providing interesting information about the plant and animal life in this desert.

Details: As you enter Indian Cove Campground, turn right at the three-way junction. The road will bend to the left and reach another junction. Turn right again (W) and drive 0.25 miles to the end parking loop and the trailhead. A short spur trail leads to the loop portion of the trail. Turn right and follow the loop around. Several intersecting trails will be encountered; follow the signage, keeping to the left. The trail will enter a large wash after 0.2 miles, turning left (S) and traveling upstream in the wash for 300 yards. Keep an eye out for the trail exiting the wash on its left side (E). Once back on firm ground, the trail leads back to the parking lot 250 yards away. Turn right at the spur trail connecting to the parking lot.

Sculpted granite and pools of water reflecting the towering granite walls of the Wonderland.

RATTLESNAKE CANYON PICNIC AREA

This parking and picnic area is located near the mouth of Rattlesnake Canyon, in the southeast corner of Indian Cove. Day-use picnic sites, complete with concrete tables and barbeques, can be found scattered around a small one-way loop. Restrooms and a Backcountry Board can also be found here. The trailhead for Rattlesnake Canyon is on the east side of the loop, next to the restroom, and the mouth of Rattlesnake Canyon lies to the east of the picnic area.

HIKE

Rattlesnake Canyon - #47

Total distance: 2.4 miles (round trip)
Physical difficulty: 4
Technical difficulty: 4
Navigating: 3
Trail type: wash travel/cross-country

Rattlesnake Canyon is without a doubt one of the most beautiful locations in all of Joshua Tree National Park. The canyon cuts deeply into the heart of the Wonderland of Rocks, leading into the densest collections of granite rocks in the Park. Towering mountains of rock line the wash on all sides. Rattlesnake Canyon serves as the predominant drainage for the entire Wonderland, and it's not uncommon to find both running water and pools for much of the year. Eons of flash-flooding have sculpted the bedrock, carving channels, potholes, grooves, flutes, and even a slickrock slot canyon. Boulders caught in the wash have been carved and polished by the ephemeral liquid. The canyon also has sections of deep sand, rooting clusters of

mesquite, juniper, piñon pine, and even a few cottonwood trees.

The "trail" is a mishmash of cross-country travel, ever-changing washes, and just walking through the canyon. The adventure starts by walking up a deep, sandy wash, weaving through and over polished, unusual boulders. Eventually the wash will enter a sea of rocks, bending around a rocky knoll and ending at a large, low-angle granite dome. This area at the base of the dome has several large natural tanks that retain water (oftentimes putrid) for much of the year, with a beautiful slot canyon/waterfall cut into the dome above. To the right of the slot, the trail ascends the dome. This section is steep, strenuous, and slightly dangerous. At the top of the dome, the wash resumes. Beautifully sculpted bedrock can be observed in this area, deeply grooved with pools, potholes, and tanks. Warning: Do not attempt to walk too close to the top of the slot canyon, the rock here is very slippery and a fall could result in serious injury or worse! As you continue up the wash, more sculpted and fluted bedrock can be seen—and felt—as several terraces have to be surmounted to continue on. Once round the final bend, the true enormity of the Wonderland of Rocks is revealed: the mass of granite domes and boulders piles and piles to a highpoint, the Ivory Tower, standing like a beacon on the futhest peak in view.

Above: Looking back at 29 Palms and the desert to the north.
Middle: Sculpted pothole and pools of water.

The upper section of Rattlesnake Canyon, which travels straight as an arrow on nearly flat ground, is the reward for all the effort! The quiet canyon echoes birdsong. Tall grasses, mesquite, piñon pine, and cottonwoods grow alongside the wash. Clusters of house-sized black

boulders offer shade and cool cubbies to explore. The faint trickle of water can often be heard as rainwater ever-so-slowly drains out of the mass of Wonderland of Rocks. Bighorn sheep are known to come down out of the rocky labyrinth in late afternoons and wee hours of the morning, cautiously drinking from the many pools in the canyon.

Rattlesnake Canyon eventually chokes off some 1.2 miles from the parking loop, in a cluster of large boulders that becomes too dense to tunnel and climb through. Look to the left (S) here; it's possible to hike over a notch and find your way south to Willow Hole (Hike #4, page 46), but this very adventurous link-up is beyond the scope of this book.

Details: Park at the Backcountry Board on the east side of the Rattlesnake Parking Loop. Restrooms can be found here. Walk the trail east from the board, through a small forest of creosote bushes to the deep, sandy wash. Turn right (S) and head up the wash. This section of the wash requires climbing over and around many boulders. Observe some interesting "mega-cryst" quartz in the boulders. Eventually the rocks will let up and the wash will bend to the right (SW) before sweeping back to the left in a large semi-circle. The wash will then dead-end at a section of pools, troughs, and polished boulders. Exit via the sand on the right side, then ascend the rock hillside, which turns into the long slope of a granite dome. A slot canyon/waterfall will be to the left of the ascent path. The long slope will soon pinch down to a small canyon and a groove. Shimmy under an oak tree and surmount a 5-foot-tall shelf. After that, the small canyon opens up at a summit. Veer left a bit, downclimbing a small terrace of slickrock to regain the wash. Turn right, and follow the wash upstream for about 400 yards. The wash becomes rocky once again, requiring a bit of crawling/climbing/shimmying to navigate. Look for a faint trail on the right side of the wash, which travels beneath a huge boulder and then along the top of a small cliff band. Several small terraces have to be negotiated here to continue on. Once past the terraces, the wash bends to the right (W) and becomes easy walking for the remainder. Continue down the large wash for another 0.5 miles, wandering through several clusters of boulders en route. The hike ends at an impassable pile of boulders that fills the west end of the wash. Return as you came.

Above left: Water, tall grasses, and a cottonwood tree found near the end of Rattlesnake Canyon.
Below: Tadpoles in the desert!

Above: Palms at 49 Palms Oasis, some showing signs of a past fire.

49 PALMS OASIS

The 49 Palms Oasis is a fine little adventure located just outside of the town of 29 Palms. A moderately strenuous 1.5-mile hike leads from the parking lot out to the oasis. Several nice stands of California Fan Palms can be found at the oasis, as well as intermittent pools of water. The short road leading into the area and the parking lot both have rock outcroppings and boulders that are worthy of exploration. In addition, enjoy excellent views of 29 Palms and the surrounding desert.

To reach the 49 Palms parking lot: On Highway 62 at the west end of the town of 29 Palms, turn south on Canyon Road and drive 0.8 miles. There, the road will bend left and become Forty-Nine Palms Canyon Road, shortly thereafter entering Joshua Tree National Park. The road will end at the parking loop a grand total of 1.8 miles from the highway. Restrooms can be found at the parking lot.

HIKE

49 Palms Oasis - #48

Total distance: 7 miles (round trip)
Physical difficulty: 3
Technical difficulty: 2
Navigating: 2
Trail type: official trail

The 49 Palms Oasis is a beautiful oasis tucked away at the mouth of a deep canyon. At the oasis, several mature stands of California Fan Palms grow along the base of a substantial spring. Pools of water can be found tucked in beneath the boulders below the palms. Seen from afar, the lush green foliage and inviting shade of the oasis makes a stark contrast to the barren, steep mountains that surround it.

Top: Stunning vistas on the trail to the 49 Palms Oasis. Looking north at the town of 29 Palms and the 29 Palms Marine Base beyond.
Above: The oasis as seen on the approach.

The trail leading out is somewhat vigorous, rising steeply from the parking lot into the hills and then dropping down even further into the canyon behind. Views from the initial hills are outstanding, including the 49 Palms Oasis, the town of 29 Palms, and the desert beyond. Vibrant red barrel cactus dot the hillsides, contrasting nicely with the dark rocks of the hills. Descending into the canyon behind the hills is a bit steep, with some loose rock—and about a thousand man-made steps! The steps may be murder on the knees, but they seem to be stabilizing the hillside. Once at the oasis, several small trails weave through the brush and under the trees, including one that travels up the canyon on the right (S), leading to

Right: Tall grasses and reeds grow out of standing water at the heart of the oasis.

Above: If you continue above the 49 Palms Oasis, many slickrock catchments and pools of water can be found. Oftentimes, small waterfalls link the pools together.

intermittent pools of water in slickrock.

It should be noted that several visitors each year are rescued from along this hike, typically the result of heat exhaustion or overexertion. There is no escaping the intense sun on this hike! Bring plenty of water and remember that the return hike is actually more strenuous than the hike in.

Details: From the parking lot, take the obvious trail south. The trail will weave through some rocks, then ascend the hillside. After several difficult switchbacks, the angle eases and the trail winds over the hilltop. Once over the hill, the oasis comes into view. After sufficiently gazing at the immaculate views in every direction, continue on the trail. It first descends gently, then steepens into what used to be a rutted mess and is now a thousand steps. After descending for quite a way, the trail reaches a dry wash, weaving through rocks and over a small hill before reaching the oasis.

Above: Strange rocks in the canyon above 49 Palms Oasis must have a fascinating geological story to tell. Shredded granitic rock laced with marble-like inclusions?

Above: A second oasis can be found a half mile up the canyon behind 49 Palms Oasis; a single fan palm sits among a dense thicket of mesquite. This is a hard-earned view!
Below: A late-afternoon rainbow forms over the mountains above the 49 Palms Oasis.

INDEX

Bold - Chapter
Green - Hikes
Burgundy - Picnic Areas
Dark Blue - Maps

Notes:

Robert Miramontes first visited Joshua Tree National Park in the mid 1980s as a young and impressionable teenager. While there, he witnessed rock climbers scaling the sheer cliff walls and vowed to never engage in the sport. Well, several years later, Rob found himself back in the Park doing the unthinkable—rock climbing! This marked the beginning of a life-long obsession with Joshua Tree National Park. Initially, with rock climbing as the focus, he set out to explore every crag and rock pile, every cliff and summit. This culminated in the writing of four rock-climbing books for the area. During this time, Rob cultivated another passion, photography. Combining these two passions led to the creation of this book. Robert lives in nearby Desert Hot Springs with his wife Christina and their three-year-old daughter Alexandra.